# THE GRACE OF
# BLACK MOTHERS

# The Grace of
# Black Mothers

by Martheaus Perkins

Copyright © July 1, 2025 by Martheaus Perkins

No part of this book may be used or performed without written consent of the author, if living, except for critical articles or reviews.

Perkins, Martheaus
1st edition

ISBN: 978-1-949487-42-8
Library of Congress Control Number: 2024947142

Interior design by Hadley Hendrix
Cover design by Baonhia Xiong
Cover art by B. Broadie
Primary Editing by Natasha Kane
Supporting Editing by Ali Shafer

Trio House Press, Inc.
Minneapolis
www.triohousepress.org

*To every badass Mom*

# Table of Contents

## Act I: Coup de Grâce

| | |
|---|---|
| Family Album | 14 |
| Pros and Cons for Keeping the Baby | 15 |
| Scene from a Center, Texas Walmart | 16 |
| Black Mom | 20 |
| Another Poem About Trayvon Martin | 21 |
| The Verdict | 23 |
| Jaden Smith Stole Our Role in *The Karate Kid* | 24 |
| American Dream with the Help of Morphine | 25 |
| my | 29 |
| I Miss Your Stories | 30 |
| Houston, Texas | 32 |
| Sutures in Our Photos | 33 |
| Captions for Pictures Lost in Storage | 34 |
| Secret Identity | 37 |
| Every Brown Child Turns 18 and Asks their White Father for a Tattoo | 38 |
| Paintings She Made in Rehab | 40 |
| Howl for Momma Rat | 41 |

**Act II: Airs & Graces**

Girl     46

Truth is Unpronounceable by Itself     47

7 Tips for Installing a Cheap Tombstone for Granny (Under $639)     49

Notes on a Poem I Wrote at Twelve     51

Which Batman Villain Is Your Deadbeat Dad?     53

Streaming Dreams Where Mom Didn't Have a Baby     56

Optometry with Momma     58

The [     ] Dream Has a Baby in a Prison [     ]     60

Footstool Sister     61

Scene from the Reading     63

Scholarship Letter     65

Aiyana Mo'Nay Stanley-Jones Picks a College Major     66

They Were Killed Holding     67

Mamie Till-Mobley's Reddit Post     68

All the Black Mothers in America Hold a Press Conference     69

The [American] Dream Has a Baby in a Prison [Hospital]     70

my     71

**Act III: Saving Grace**

Southern Hymns     74

FATALITY!     75

| | |
|---|---|
| The Welfare Queen Pyrate Code | 77 |
| Dear Swiss Rolls | 79 |
| Ode to Toaster Ovens | 80 |
| Grace Must Be | 81 |
| Dominoes | 82 |
| Church Jewelry and Mourning Dead Words | 83 |
| Mothers Singing Their Souls Out | 85 |
| Amazing Grace | 86 |
| Beyoncé, a Black Man Wants to Tell You | 87 |
| Back When We Danced | 88 |
| A Dream's Child | 89 |
| Three Black Sons, Three Black Mothers | 90 |
| After Visiting Jasper, Texas | 91 |
| my | 92 |
| An American Dream's Night Stroll | 93 |
| The Grace of Black Mothers | 94 |
| Center, Texas | 95 |
| Scene from the Rehab Center | 96 |
| *Notes* | 101 |
| *Gratitude* | 103 |
| *About the Author* | 105 |
| *About the Artist* | 107 |
| *Artist Statement: About the Cover Art* | 109 |

"There still remains the question regarding the role of and impact on Black mothers during matters of institutional violence against Black children . . . Black women are subject to terror from police and system agents, they face reproductive justice issues, as they are criminalized as mothers—and are affected mentally, but they employ various resistance strategies that strengthen their resilience.
Results indicate that Black women are the backbone and martyrs of their communities, but this comes at a tremendous cost . . ."

> – Leah Iman Aniefuna, M. Amari Aniefuna,
> & Jason M. Williams, from *Women & Criminal Justice*

# Act I

# Coup de Grâce

*When I was your age, Mar Mar, I could bust a move.*

**Family Album**

Balancing a cherry Twizzler
between bony fingers
imitating Momma's cigarettes.
Not sure if I'm intruding
on black and white lives
or being invited to sit with cousins,
sopping pancakes in Mrs. Butterworth's,
interrupted by Polaroid ticks.

I'll lie on their long and boxy
Fleetwood Cadillac hoods like a twin bed.
Fight sleep as they tell stories about dancehalls,
road trips with sunroofs left at home,
what my mom and her mom
were like when they were my age.

I see them here.
Momma and Ne Ne.
They've never looked more
like mother and daughter,
both too young. Both smile
at the future they'd hate to meet

**Pros and Cons for Keeping the Baby**

*from Momma's Journal*

| Cons | Pros |
|---|---|
| • I'll be a grandmom by 40—maybe 50 if I raise him right.<br>• Drill team. Damn, they need me too cause Hannah has trigger toe. She's 20 and thinks she can still ballet on the side. That girl should know that's only for toothpicks and 5-year-olds.<br>• If I drop a pen, I'll look like Humpty Dumpty picking it up. But no king's men are coming to pick my black ass pieces off the concrete.<br>• I don't see myself as a big girl.<br>• I'll have to tell Mom. Maybe she'll be able to take care of him while I finish college.<br>• I can tell this is going to be one heavy ass baby, and I have bad knees.<br>• I'd have to be his mother and father. I don't think Tre is serious enough about stepping up as a stepdad. He plays too much anyway.<br>• Jessica said she'd let me have the dorm, but I'll miss crying in her lap and MTV Thursdays.<br>• He could grow up to be a little shit. If he's anything like me, I'll pull my hair out.<br>• This wasn't the plan. I can take a break after my Associates and come back to finish my accounting certificate—shit. Loans. Loans. Loans.<br>• I'm still a child myself. | • I love him already. |

### Scene from a Center, Texas Walmart

*Blackout. POET stands in the stage wing shadows. Loose-screwed wheels of shopping carts, early 2000s Tim McGraw intercom tunes, and bovine Texan chatter. Curtain rises with lights. Center, Texas' pride and joy, Walmart, is bustling with Sunday sundress belles, gap-toothed preschoolers in clip-on ties, and beer-bellied fathers in their cleanest collared shirts. MOTHER enters stage right pushing a shopping cart with BABY POET, passing OLD MAN BUCK, who stares a little too long.*

**MOTHER**
(tickling newborn) Say hello to Mr. Buck, Mar Mar. (pushing cart stage left) Now, let's get you some milk.

*MOTHER is here for her use-it-or-lose-it "Women, Infants, and Children" benefits from the state. She dangles through the dairy aisle like a chain is holding her posture. These are some of the first Centerites BABY POET has ever seen. MOTHER is held up with the knowledge that she made one hell of a baby. From the fruit bins to the baby wipe section, she's greeted with enough "awws" and "look at hims" to itch her scarred stomach. Though, when she notices shoppers squinting and sending loose-mouth stares her way, it feels like she's been miscast. MOTHER enters the check-out line. She recognizes the CASHIER from high school. They graduated a year ago together.*

**CASHIER**
(eyebrows reaching her hairline) Thea! Whose baby is— (doing mental math). I heard you were pregnant. Girl—he is so handsome!

**MOTHER**
(restraining herself) Hey, Ashley! This is Martheaus. I just had him, actually. How have you been, girl?

**CASHIER**

Saving for college (scanning formula). You? (eyeing BABY POET)

**MOTHER**

Trying. Doing what I can, you know? Thinking about going back to T.J.C. once we get situated.

*After being checked out, MOTHER rolls stage right to the store exit. Enter OLD ASS LADY, clad in pounds of costume jewelry, dry rosemary perfume, and plastic bags of applesauce, traipsing to meet MOTHER and BABY POET near the 15-cent Granny Smiths.*

**OLD ASS LADY**

(seeing BABY POET and losing her shit, starts warbling. Waddles toward MOTHER like a blue jean peacock) Oh my goodness! Look at him—he's precious! Oh lord, he's precious!

**MOTHER**

Thank—

**OLD ASS LADY**

Look at those little toes! How old is he?

**MOTHER**

Two months.

**BABY POET**

(babying).

**OLD ASS LADY**

He is the sweetest little thang. Whose is he?

**MOTHER**

(Let's hope you've cast the right mother. She'll need to play this one as delicate as an orchid petal) He's mine, ma'am.

                          **OLD ASS LADY**
(wraps her hand around the front of MOTHER's shopping
cart, laughs like Lindsey Graham: dainty plantation
spice). No. No, this baby can't be yours, sweetie. He's
white.

                              **MOTHER**
No, he's mine.

                          **OLD ASS LADY**
Now quit that, girl. This here ain't your baby. Whose is
it really?

                              **MOTHER**
He's mine. I have the scar to prove it (starts pushing
cart).

> OLD ASS LADY lurches her hands toward BABY POET,
> trying to unhook his seat. MOTHER swats at her wrin-
> kled claws and pushes the cart forward. She won't
> budge.

                          **OLD ASS LADY**
All these abandoned kids out here and you decide to steal
<u>this</u> baby. You're not leaving, no—I won't allow it.

                              **MOTHER**
Didn't steal this one. You need to move away.

                          **OLD ASS LADY**
You stay right here, I'm calling the law. (gesturing to
CASHIER) Keep this girl here, I have to call the law—she
stole someone's baby.

> MOTHER takes BABY POET from the seat and pats his
> butt at a heartbeat's pace to soothe them both. OLD
> ASS LADY Motorolas the police, blocking the exit.
> CASHIER leaves to get the manager. BABY POET coos
> until the POET gives him a signal offstage.

**BABY POET**
(mulling the air, cries so newborn, they sound like amniotic fluid in his vocal cords) I'm sorry for being your contraband, for the incredulous teachers, friend's parents, and old-ass ladies who wouldn't have matched us in the color game. But you are my mother, and you've left your prints on me like Crisco stains in a family cookbook.

> OFFICER DAVIS enters as a Black man, quashing OLD ASS LADY'S war march. He knows the MOTHER: an old family friend.

**OFFICER DAVIS**
This is her baby, ma'am.

**OLD ASS LADY**
I can't believe it. That baby is as white as can be—and look at her.

**POET**
(stepping out) It was somewhere around here that my mother became more than a Black girl with a white baby. I'd like to think she proved to herself that I was her son.

> OLD ASS LADY scurries off stage. MOTHER adorns BABY POET'S head with applesauce and raises him to Pride Rock—to the huddled Center-ite masses.

**MOTHER**
I've given up too much for this boy to have somebody say he isn't mine. (toughening) Next one of you who comes at us, I'm slapping the teeth out your gums.

Curtain closes. But there is still the faint drone of lies.

**Black Mom**
> *after Jericho Brown*

Be warned, I have a Black mother on my side.
She's built to whoop ass, so you better hide.

        She whipped my ass and I couldn't hide.
        "Eviction" is a word I learned at five.

Evict is the verb five boyfriends taught.
In spring, promises to your child die.

        Your promises die with a spring child.
        Bruised tongue on coal; Black moms spit flame.

Spit on, bruised—Mom's tongue blackens to coal.
Dream of Black metamorphosis, sprouting bug eyes; parts

        of a Black bug sprouting into morphed dreams. Eye
        your burden-branded son. In a different life, I

didn't brand your life. A Black son is a burden.
Be warned, Black mother. You're on my side.

## Another Poem About Trayvon Martin

Forget the Skittles, the Arizona Iced Tea, the hoodie.
You already know the verdict.

His father's beard is white now.
It's been ten years since "Up to No Good

on Drugs or Something" was followed
by Neighborhood Watch Captain—

Since "He Looks Black" was killed by
Curious Concrete-Smashed George.

"These Assholes, They Always Get Away" would have been
27 today. As old as "Not Guilty" when he murdered him.

We've soaked the roots red already,
When will the ground be ours to stand on?

Here's another one where they follow us.
Another poem for Emmett, Eric, Michael,

Tamir, Philando, Ahmaud,
George, Breonna, and—today,

Daunte Wright. His mother's clip is on TV this morning.

It's been a year since Officer "I Grabbed the Wrong
Fucking Gun" forgot which hip her taser was on.

Mrs. Wright says, *I have to be the voice of myself,*
*my family, my community—but most of all, I have*

*to be the voice of my son Daunte.*
*They left him on the ground for hours.*

*As people all over the world watched,*
*I had to cry from behind a caution tape.*

Sybrina Fulton donated Trayvon's flight suit
to the Smithsonian—he wanted to be an astronaut.

She founded "the club no one wants to be a part of."
A Circle of Mothers who set school photos of their children

next to street signs—who give victim statements to pronounce
unpronounceable grief—who can never stop being mothers.

Mamie Till opened Emmett's casket for any article, photo, or poem.
She scraped a voice from this country's taut throat.

Here's another poem about the Trayvon Martins
and the graceless way our country unmothers them.

**The Verdict**

I could've been a pajama pants poet
finding consonance in the pine trees
with a Jack Russell asleep at my feet.
        Then, I learned I was Black.
        *George Zimmerman found not guilty.*

I came this close to Neo Pastoralism—
to birds in every line that may or may not
symbolize cagelessness and virginity.
        But the picture box stamped
        "Black" on my tongue and ears.
        *E V E R Y W O R D Y O U S A Y*
        *I S F R O M / FOR A BLACK THROAT.*

*Lord, it's a shame*, Ne Ne said, lathering my scalp
in BB Oil Moisturizer. She braided stories and truth
into my tender skull: *That could've been you—*
*Promise me to watch. Be careful—know what you look like.*
        Poof. Bye bye postmodernist verse.
        You're Black now. And there's no
        time to spit on the dictionary's
        leather loafers. It's time to resist,
        Black Boy. Learn to breathe gas.

Maybe one day, I can write about jamming plastic bottles
in my Huffy's spokes to make it sound like a dirt bike.
        But not now. Not since I learned that we can't
        scrub the suspicious off our skin for these people—
        that little Black boys and girls dissolve and disappear.
        Swallowed. Minced. Spit up. You get it.
        Nothing a poem can make pretty.

**Jaden Smith Stole Our Role in *The Karate Kid***

Let us catch yo' light-skinned ass on The Great Wall of China again.
We'll show you some *real* tender-headed Black boy Kung Fu;
   drag our knuckles
      across concrete riverbanks
         of pitch and soot to bust your bottom lip.
Come clad in those ugly-ass NASCAR track pants—
that tight-ass wife-beater tank top,
that wide-ass grease-tinted forehead you got from Daddy.
Our tiger palms will Cadillac turn
   on their
      way
         to slap
            the Black off you.
We're owed a swan kick, Jaden—
owed Jackie Chan hijinks, and Bruce Li's gi.
*Our* single mom was meant to grindstone rusty spoons
into mirror-cool silver. *WE* were meant to wax and wane
in the ruby glow of lantern-lifted destiny!
Those were *OUR* fucking forbidden fruits to forage
from the Beijing Beverly Hill Chinaberry trees.

Sure, we were only twelve. And, upon reflection,
we can see how you would've been a bigger box office draw.
But can you blame us for the jealousy?

Do you have any idea how important Kung Fu is to broke Black kids?
Aching
   to pinch
      bullets
         from the breeze
or weave some semblance of control within the fibers of our futures.

When you air-balled, breakdanced, let that giggling girl
pluck strands from your hair; when castor oil drooled
from your nunchuck braids onto the pavement,
when bullies stove your stomach in,
*tell us*, where'd you summon those tears from?

## American Dream with the Help of Morphine

It's a universal rule that no one gives a damn about your dreams,
so, I'll add explosions:

The mothers of America have just flipped their first pancake;
its white scent twirls around each mother's apron and slithers
around the kitchen corner to lure out sleeping children. Only,
instead of levitating tiny princes and princesses out of bed,
the scent returns barefoot Black men in beige potato sack diapers.
Across the nation, behind the many white-fenced veils of suburbia,
this Dream hears "*Soo-wee*, dat smells fine," then
the mothers' screams, then "Ma'am, I don't means any harm," then
flying frying pans at the men, then "Alls I wants issa little help,"
and finally, "Get the fuck out of my house!"
as the moms sweep them away.
The Dream finds something better to do. *\*\*CLICK\*\**

> Anderson Cooper is on. His Ralph Lauren
> is sweat-soaked, but his hair is still perfect.
>> "We're getting reports that strange men—
>> I'm hearing they're in rags—
> He's frantic—not even looking at the camera,
>> "Strange men appearing out of nowhere!
>> Thousands, at least. This is unbelievable."
> A black man taps on Coop's shoulder and says,
>> "Massa, where is I?"

*\*\*BZZZ\*\**

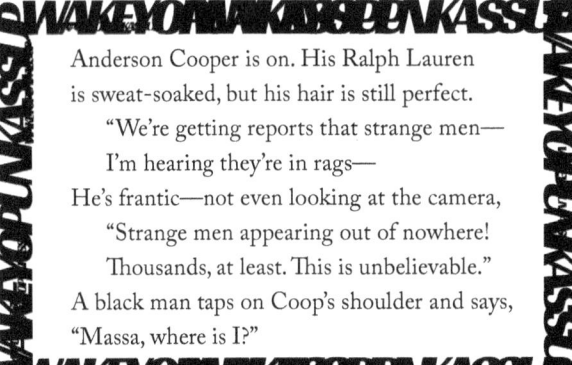

> Tucker Carlson, with an aluminum-stiff scowl,
> arms waving like a disturbed bat
> screeches slurs:
>> "Monkeygoons, Mud Apes, Black Roaches."
> He slams his boiling fist on the news desk,
>> "We're being overrun by woke, time-
>> traveling, rape-oholic, groomer, baboons!
>> And it's your Christian duty to—"

**OURBONESBENEATHOURBONESBENEATH**

HGTV. The Black people work the spacious front yard of a cozy modern visa, nestled in the heart of the (secluded) Virginia wilderness that Stacey and Dylan have dreamed to own. One brave Black man swan dives into the heated pool—the ash from his legs and winter twigs from his ropey hair float to the surface. Even though it fits the budget, Stacey was hoping for a place with a bit more character.

**OURBONESBENEATHOURBONESBENEATH**

\*\**SUUSSHH*\*\*

Nothing good is on TV these days.

**AMERICAN NIGHTMARE AMERICAN NIGHTMARE**

Whoopi Goldberg argues with the token conservative on The View. "Cages—really? You're not seriously defending caging these people—my people!" The Dream recognizes this *I could slap a bitch* energy; Momma gets this way. Conservative Barbie Girl winces, "Whoopi! I never said I was okay with cages, but I mean, come on—these slaves can't just roam around unwatched. Think of the example we're setting for the children." The silly-haired one injects, "They're 'enslaved persons,' Alyssa, not slaves." Whoopi summons a dark rage, "I bet you wouldn't have a problem if they were bleach-skinned, dammit!"

**AMERICAN NIGHTMARE AMERICAN NIGHTMARE**

Harriet Tubman smashes the Dream's TV with a cattle whip,
    "Listen, follow, live!"
She injects the veins with a morphine soliloquy
"We blazed across the entrails of this land, had to come up
with our own lantern light. You don't see me. You don't see us.
For your generation is bound to nightmares of deferred retribution—
bound to distractions. Like a mother's name, you inherit
my sympathies, children, for how often their motherland buries
our people's symphonies. I wish it was as simple as watching for light

waiting for a hoot owl call. But you gotta get up off your asses. Don't docile. Hell was whatever direction my back faced. But that screen tricks you into plunging toward it."
    The Dream asks what it should do.
Miss Tubman says, "Untie the noose around your necks."
    "What noose?" The Dream looks down—

**sssssssssssssssssssssssssssssssssssssssssssssssss**

The History Channel is on, playing through the static cracks.

> It's only them this time. Shackles loose on their dusty ankles, skin sealed taut around their ribcages, peeled lips, crust-clotted tear ducts, and a *Pawn Stars* advertisement banner in the lower left corner for the season finale at 8/7 C. They pour out of the TV, then down the Dream's eyes like liquid mercury, cooling, stiffening their blunted backs, expanding to fit the Dream's throat, hardening into metal, choking the Dream's lungs—
their sweat evaporates

into a smothering smog of iron and lead that spills over
America.
Eardrums shredded by a million snapped necks, copper cuts
along the spine—

"*The American Dream. The American Dream.*" The ghosts hymn,
"*We've never left. We've never left this American Dream.*"
And the Dream ends itself.


And there's an explosion.

**my**

# Mar.

His Granny dips her girlhood nickname in honey, honey honey honey soothes a legacy to let go honey honey Thea, honey, *let's call your son "Mar Mar"* honey honey honey honey that honey-skinned boy with a mother too young to drink honey honey honey honey honey honey and his too young grandmother who'll one day peel clumps of grief from her honey chemo scalp honey honey for letting her daughter tumble toward a rat trap honey honey honey honey honey *Thea left town with you, honey.* honey *I should've stepped up sooner* honey honey honey honey.

Mar visits his Granny's house years later playing empty stomach jazz honey honey honey lanky bone-wristed pleas to stay away from Momma Houston honey honey honey honey honey a Black woman's honey mouth simultaneously sings the loudest and weakest demands in our motherland honey honey honey honey
Granny says *I couldn't make her stay* honey honey honey honey honey honey

One visit, Mar Mar and Thea arrive for a summer-swaddled movie night with honey honey Antonio Banderas's saber-sharp timbre slashing blazing Zs on honey outlaws and oil barons "*so the devil will know*" who sent them Hellward honey honey honey honey honey Momma and Granny on stage together honey honey finally honey honey honey honey honey strapping a strawberry-laced quilt cape loose around Mar's honey daydreams honey honey honey That hour, he had both his mothers. Until

## I Miss Your Stories

Ne Ne, like your best Sunday dress, you start to fade.
Gem-laced peplum, splashed with mushroom beige—
that time your grandbaby upchucked his applesauce—
grainy, powdered hurl all over those pearls.

   Tell me, Ne Ne, about that time you lost your class.
   Took a box cutter to that man's forehead—
   carved your initials 'cause he cussed you bad.
   Ends with your pearl-handled pistol jamming—
   a crooked cop you almost shot.

      Ne Ne, there's the one with my aunties.
      Nappy-haired runaways
      didn't get past the liquor store. A scared momma
      squeezing a tattered belt for all its worth.
      Auntie Shawn doesn't tell it like you.

      Ne Ne, it's murmurs down a washburned tunnel
      like the time your sister tricked you
      down the water-wrapped underpass.
      Closed in while the sea sat on top.
      Cadillacs shouldn't turn to submarines.
      *Get me.*
      *the hell.*
      *out of here.*
      you said.

      Got any new jokes?
      The old ones' punchlines
      land limp-fisted—
      swollen soft.
      Not the same, Ne Ne. No
      dominoes on that shabby fold-out table. No

            flying down backroads with Ben E. King
            *Supernatural* as we can be.

Here's a passport photo of you and Auntie Shawn.
   Raising children since you were a child, and
   I never knew you left the country, and
   I'm sorry, Ne Ne, and I'm sorry, Ne Ne, and
   I'm sorry, Ne Ne, for never asking,
                                  tell me.
                                  —tell me.

## Houston, Texas

Momma, we were rats in Houston,
our tails caught in the gutters of Tidwell.
We sipped chunks of sewage, nibbled
at gray meat stuck to the bones
of Two-Piece Tuesday chicken. We hid
from light bills in cramped pantries,
rested under eviction notices
like blankets made for sweating.
We lived like litter, discarded
by Cypress, then Antoine Dr.,
then Humble, then South Side.
No skyscraper shade for us
as we wore our soles
out on miles of concrete
sidewalks. 87-minute walks
from Antoine to Langfield—
school bus wouldn't touch
our ward: more liquor stores
than restaurants. We walked
streets like cartographers
of poverty.
Our Houston was a cockroach
crawling out of my backpack at
Katherine Smith Elementary,
Our Houston is the abandoned
Dairy Queen where stamps sold
for blunts or a son's bike.
Our Houston was peppermint Metros
stopping at graffitied cracked windows.
Our Houston was *pack your suitcases, Mar,*
*we can't stay here anymore, Mar.*
Our Houston was six homes and five schools
in four years.
Our Houston was no place for boys
to be                                          raised.

                                        You love it there.

## Sutures in Our Photos

Momma, let's stitch the lesions men left on our lives—repeat
  photos together   the two of us   undoing years
of our bliss, our dreams   disappear when we're   working to forget
  our truths;   too afraid to heal   our history.

  In this photo,   you pretended to wish on   one man.
you let canola oil spark   white stars   spit
  from the pan—   plenty of youth   on you.

  We danced   to deflect   dangerous men
  like cockroaches   being stomped,   crushed,
  scattered   by backhands,   our bodies
over the floor.

  Here's one where   they left   meth behind
your white teeth—   dried tear ducts and   their words
were enough to make   treads   luring you
    home.

**Captions for Pictures Lost in Storage**

Christmas 2009. Mar Mar is seven. Still into Star Wars!! I got him Mace Windu's lightsaber because I like purple. Didn't know it made noises though ): Kept me up all night, but my baby is happy!!

2010. My boyfriend Don playing Xbox with Mar Mar. Some racing game. Mar's head is only half cornrows because he started crying. He's tender-headed like me. Don told him to man up and it didn't go too well! Don is the yellow Ferrari on the TV (aka the one getting his ass kicked in fourth place).

First day of middle school—he's sprouting like a weed. We're at the "Young Men's College Preparatory Academy." Had to scrape scrape scrape to get him this school uniform, but he is so precious in his khakis and blazer.

Halloween 2010. Count Blackula! He came up with that name, don't know where he picked that up from. He gets to trick or treat at our Riverbrook (old) and the new apartment this year. Not much candy, but he said he wanted to see his friends one last time before we had to move again.

2011. Mar Mar riding in the backseat of Terry's car with his favorite Legos. He's been silent because we had to put away a few things in storage. We made sure he could fill a backpack of toys before we left them all. Mar was sad, but I told him we could come up and switch out when he gets tired of those. Plus, they won't be in there long. Has his hair like Qui Gon Jinn—fav hairstyle and fav Jedi.

Mar and Momma cheesing at Dairy Queen. She came down to get him. Soooo happy about her just showing up out of nowhere. Mar is ecstatic about going to live with his Ne Ne. Happy he's happy. But we had it just fine up here. Just going to take this time to get on my feet. We'll look back at this and laugh. He's trying the Belt Buster burger for the first time. This boy can eat away at anything. 2012

July 2006 — I scraped enough to buy a little tonka truck     He wanted to roll his chest into cement,   become a superhero for us.
Cement Man can build a house on loose sediment. He can harden his knuckles, black eyes buried in cement   they won't harden if we keep moving     and we keep moving—we're building something I don't deserve on my own.

2007 December 6th. Mar's new suit! He's clipped his tie on himself. He says he wants to be a businessman when he grows up so he can buy me a house. He has a stern look when he tells me—like my credit score is carved on the raw skin of my forehead—like he knows what I do to tie us down. But he can't know. He can't know. He can't.

35

My 21st birthday party. Momma took Mar for the night so I could have some time for myself.

4/11/2002. 4:12am. A boy. I can't lift my arms, so he is draped over them like a stone ribbon. *Keep your eyes shut*, I tell him. *I don't want you to see me.* I thought he'd be warmer. I furnaced myself—ate diary pages and denied applications for kindling. He has egg skin. Hatched, boiled, cracked.

**Secret Identity**

You said *son* with an untuned fiddle's twang;
black canary cuts to a six-year-old boy's ears.
I said Spider-Man was my favorite superhero.

*'Cause he ain't got no daddy?*

Sorry, my skin was too chill-snapped to giggle at quips
in your rust-lined Ford Ranger. I'd forgotten my puffy,
Hulk-muscle coat. If only I was pissed or had a serum,
I could've grown to match your spruce-needle face.
You were proud of my new light-up Sketchers,
and I tried to Professor X your mind—
find a secret identity under your sunglasses and cap.

I never knew why Momma was angry the morning
of that team-up. But last week, she told me you said,
*If I have to pay for him, I want to get a look at him.*
Silence was more honest than the dress-up words.

You draped your faded denim jacket over my back—
and I wish this metaphor could be a cape,
but it landed jagged and weakened my shoulders.

Was I your son there?
Dad's jacket wrapping me
in make-believe superpowers.

**Every Brown Child Turns 18 and Asks their White Father for a Tattoo**

Dad, I know how you love laughing at your jokes. So . . . what if it were
a macho man savagely eating a bowl of chili tatted on the soft lines
of our tattered biceps? His barnacled tongue could sweep down like a sleeve.
                                        *Naaaaaa.* Not pretty enough.
How about a butterfly chasing dandelion seeds above our battered scalps—
sending down inky wires to make us dance. Marionette strings of ink
dropping down like care packages—*well, no.* Dropping down like bombs.
                                     *Naww.* No one does solid
                                      Blackwork in our area.
Maybe just a sound?—a rattle, screech, scratch-strumming our throat cords.
How many printed screams do you think would fit on our necks?
                                         *Nooooo.*
                           Neck tats are hard to cover.
                           And none of us look good in turtlenecks.
Oh! I got it! The entirety of Kendrick Lamar's *To Pimp a Butterfly* on our
calf—all the way up to our ass cracks. And, if they have extra ink, maybe
they can plug in our bullet holes—maybe the artist can restitch the ghost to
its limbs?
                                         *Nooo.*
                       If you're going to write something
                            between your skin,
                           it can't be that obvious.
                             That *momentary. Nooo.*
                         We want lyric mysterious—
                    some shit to chew on—chew through.
                        Triple entendre in Japanese:
                    a drooping mango tree *symbolizing* . . .

How's this for a symbol, Dad:
  A brown child hopping on lily pads across this country's chest.
  They can be running from their name—Aiyana Stanley-Jones,
  Adam Toledo, Ma'Khia Bryant, Emmett Till, Trayvon Martin—
  and, now that I'm saying this out loud, maybe the lily pads can be
  the babies who were bombed—*who are bombed*—
  too young to even say their own names.

Would you like to laugh now?
  How about a Jake the Dog tramp stamp—
    a stick-and-poke Rugrats sketch across our gut?

Would you like to laugh *now*?
    Slap a knee?
     Hold your squirming stomach as you crane
       that clean skin away from the eclipse?

It really doesn't matter what we choose;
 we're only getting this tattoo because *it's our rebellious phase*.
All that matters is having that Black ink seep into our arteries—
filling our Black hearts black.

**Paintings She Made in Rehab**

I. *Still life Livingroom Speckled with Scents*
Our stench of burdens: sin, cocoa butter,
hints of pinewood. Suffocates my mouth
with a plastic bag gas mask—when we read
these poems together, waft, don't sniff.
Intricate tea leaves I tried to read
from drug smoke hsking through a roach room.

II. *Untitled Surrealist Landscape*
Why is abstract art so natural for the black-and-blue hand to paint,
Momma? Why can this canvas not hold every cigarette scorch mark
ashed by our story? Why can I not say what happened to us without
breaking away? So much open landscape to unburden yourself through
the baby. The Black boy derailing the plan. New leather tires licking
the freeway until they get popped. You should've clipped the hang nail.

III. *An Equation for Statistic Siblings*
While we try to convince a hurricane we matter, more mangling.
Those kids were supposed to graduate college.
Momma, you were supposed to be an accountant.
This art was supposed to be true, but it's an inoperable
answer. On one side of the equal line, tallies of starved bodies. The other,
splatters of gold-platted stomachs. On one side of the equal line, a howling
mother trying to express an infinity. The other,

IV. *Family Portrait of the American Dream* (unfinished)
You had so much potential before me.
Not enough time to finish being a daughter
before sketching yourself as a mother.
In your piece, the many Dream Children spatter
the foreground. White forefathers stockpile at the frame's edge.
One Black mother holds center gaze but averts her eyes.

## Howl for Momma Rat

    I saw the dreaming lungs of my Black mother's youth
Kush and Crown-laced; crossing tennis shoe powerline beltways
    to find oxytocin for her central amygdala—
        to scavenge money for my schooling.
    Rat-bodied ballerina, she twirls top-heavy into the arms of anyone
who can squeeze—ring out the last ounces of brown-sacked liquor
        in the cracking cement of her mind.
My little sister's name was Meth; Momma taught her makeup
    on a tiled floor—
tipsy on taking the memories away. *Stuff cotton in my mandible;*
*make it all pretty, Baby Girl.*
    She was our coup de grâce:
No, Momma can't survive without a pipe to keep your son's future alive.
    No, Momma can't leave Pete or Don or Jerry or the skittering mattresses
        or Raymond or the exterminator landlords or the musician;
            he showed me how to roll a blunt while you were out working.
            His old hands and fried voice were like the dads' on TV.

Momma Rat, could ya snap back at the cats looking for tiny snacks
    on Bellfort Avenue?
        Cheap yourself so we don't need to live under a bridge—
a few more days with him, and I can play the Xbox. A few more grins,
and we'll have a ride to Walmart.
Let's food-stamp skip through the aisles, Cinnamon Toast
    Crunch our joy into small bites.
      Meth needs diapers, and let's be happy while we don't need the suitors
—let's family together.
    Those duskdawn promises rise and rinse themselves in a pool of smoke
and bubbling bongs.

When Meth was a toddler, Momma perfected her fakestain smile.
She'd sing, *Good-hearted breeze, please don't let my little son see me.*
But I saw.
    I wanted Houston to sink in her own harbor.
    I'm Egyptian-eyed in these pictures:
    wise as pyramid dust—eight or ten years old?
        We could've fled like rats from the sinking ship,
swam toward the trees,
    but you never wanted to leave.

Hope was a rat drinking Motown-rich juice out a thimble.
*Stick with me, now, stick to me.*
                      Cigarette smoke dragged on my school uniforms.
*We worth the vow, stick to me now.*
                Even though I escaped your Stockholm town.
*City's rich with dance—just take a chance.*
                I need to say thank you.
*Stick with me, now. Stick to me.*
                    Because you did this for your children.
*Spit it out, Meth Mouth, stick with me, now.*
                    You howled for our dreams.

# Act II
# Airs & Graces

*It's okay, Mar Mar. We'll get out of this.*

**Girl**

My mother was as old as I am now when she had me: 19.
Young enough to be called *girl* in a supermarket by grey-
headed women who wore brooches and black stockings.
Sometimes I caught that girl posing in cherry wigs
and aviators for a Facebook post, jumping closed
pool fences and cannonballing herself in "6FT,"
gambling her heart on young men she never should've smiled at,
inflating Hubba Bubba into a pink astronaut helmet,
or cackle-sneezing nose milk after a well-timed fart joke.
This ounce of a girl was there and gone like a party trick.

And that would've been a sweet ending for this poem.
Glittery, hopeful, whimsy, brief, uncomplex.
Truth is, that girl was always the mother, is still the mother.
Truth is, that little girl and this little boy raised each other
with cockroach cardboard walls, playing hopscotch homes,
food-skipping our way to recess, cops and cowboys
patrolling the streets one callous mile after another,
cap guns raised skyward, getting popped upside the head
by drunk outlaw boyfriends who knew horseplay
like we knew the backs of their hands.
On our midnight street hikes to find friendly pillow forts,
the little girl said *People in Paris walk everywhere.*

Only a *girl* would see baguette-twirling mimes
and Heaven-tickling iron towers in a world
of busted lips and gutter surfing.
Truth is, she tried to convince us both.
Truth is, there's no lie a child can't imagine.

## Truth is Unpronounceable by Itself

1) I lie when I don't have to. It is natural, and fighting the natural is an unnatural act for an animal. To fight nature is to fight the eyes of my painter, who knew what shade I should be—where my smudge would go on the Grand Universe Canvas. An animal must do what an animal has been programmed to do.
   a) This is called the Naturalistic Fallacy. Its label means I am not the first to use nature as an authority.
   b) This is called an Appeal to Authority.
2) I blame the ink instead of the pen for my lies.
3) I make up words: mommaphobia, lyricification. They ask if the words are real.
   a) By *real*, they really mean dictionaryable—they mean "power-verified."
   b) The words were real when you read them, even if the words weren't real when I wrote them.
   c) Why listen to the God of Definitions, anyway? It's you and me who have the power here.
4) I'm not convinced lying and lyric-ing are separate verbs. Similes and metaphors are constituted by fragments of truth and fragments of lies. Together they make a splintered sincerity that connects reader to writer. We'll call this a lieric.
5) In a fiction writing class, I'm depressed to hear my inclusion of a character's gait *wastes words that could be used better elsewhere in the narrative*. This character is a musician who abuses his cat.
   a) I wrote, "His feet clopped on the floor like slabs of pork chops hitting a cutting board: damp steps, hefty steps, dense steps. He fee-fi-fo-fummed when he crossed the bedroom floor—pressing his hammer cloppers through the linoleum." *It's a funny detail*, Fiction Guy says, *but the way he walks has nothing to do with his character. Instead of talking about his feet, maybe talk about his hands so the reader can have a vivid symbol for the abuse.* I want to say, "But it does, Fiction Guy, '*have to do with his character.*'" But telling would be admitting to a lie.
   b) The musician isn't a fictional character. He wasn't born on the page; he was born in Louisiana. He didn't hit a cat; he hit my mother. Though, I didn't lie when I wrote his name was Pete or that—when he walked—it sounded like pork chops.
   c) Telling Workshop Guy that Nonfiction Pete spat on the author's mother because she didn't make the pork chops

right—or that the author still hears Nonfiction Pete's footsteps like hammers cracking through the kitchen floor—would be giving the game away.
6) I play a game to see how realistic I can make a lie. The game is "writing what I know." The game is painting over the truth—burying my mommaphobia in scene, plot, and image.
   a) a.k.a. lyricification.
7) I should clarify that when I wrote "ink," I meant blood. And when I wrote "pen," I meant myself.
   a) I should also clarify that by "blood" I meant heredity.
8) Momma lied when she didn't have to. I was a good son; I listened—I learned how to lie.
   a) I made Momma into a cat because animals don't lie; it's not in their nature.
   b) Now, I'm lying that Momma wasn't a liar. It's less confusing when she's a cat.
   c) I made Momma into a cat because I don't know why she didn't leave Pete sooner. I don't know why she let me hear him beat her while I shriveled on the couch downstairs.
   d) I made Momma into a cat because she is one. Because you would never blame a cat for being beaten by an abusive musician whose walk sounds like pork chops. Because she couldn't fiction her way out.
9) I lie because it is valuable to lie for the ones you love.
   a) Truth is unpronounceable by itself.
10) I lie to myself when I don't need to because I can't find Pete and shove a pork chop down his larynx. I can't "unvictimize" Momma/cat because that word isn't real.
    a) In fiction, the musician's cat gets away. The musician's cat becomes more than an object to follow an apostrophe-S. The musician is arrested for abuse and "treated like an animal" in prison. Momma/cat finds an honest home.
    b) In fiction, the writer is cured of his mommaphobia.

**7 Tips for Installing a Cheap Tombstone for Granny (Under $639)**

1. Buy Online
    What do crypto coins, bacon-flavored lingerie, 3D-printed rocket launchers, urine-powered diffusers, and gravestones have in common? You can buy them on Amazon (other retailers available)! Take advantage of that 10% off personalizedgravestones.org Facebook ad you got five days after Granny died. Virtual markets will provide your family with enough variety—in price and appearance—to fuel weeks of bickering. Note that black and white options are cheapest.
2. Size Matters
    Trust me, go for the 20-inch-wide one. This is Ne Ne we're talking about. You loved her far more than 13 inches of shitty slate. (Check out our <u>Top 5 Do It Yourself Gravestone Websites</u>).
3. Don't Burden Yourself with Logistics
    Have it delivered to your front yard.
4. Give Up
    My, my, you really screwed the dead pooch on that last tip. Now, there's a chunk of marble with Ne Ne's face staring at ash-heavy skies and falling bird shit. Go figure, you (a high school freshman), your diabetic aunts, and your tipsy mother—no matter how much cognac she's infused with—can't lift 325 pounds. Leave it for a couple of weeks; it'll give you something to wave at before catching the school bus.
5. Use a Dolly
    Dolly! You're a genius; I didn't think of that and I'm the God of Tips. Use a dolly to move the tombstone into your SUV. Remember to keep its receipt! She would've wanted you to recoup that $85. Don't worry, leaving hideous scars on the marble is expected.
    Ne Ne always said beauty was internal.
6. Create Your Own Graveyard
    If you could not raise the dolly because adding 325 pounds to a dolly makes it difficult to lift, **don't panic**. You have a *grave*stone; you have a front *yard*. I see a simple math equation. She was an introvert; maybe a private plot isn't so bad. Plus, you get to up-dig her and bring her home.
7. Contemplate Death
    Don't get too carried away. Focus on the stone—an attempt to immortalize the mortal. Stones don't get brain tumors the size of

grapefruits and die in hospice. Stones don't need their baby pebbles to order graver stones from sketchy websites. Stones match the stillness of death—the weight of it. How heavy should your stone be? Unmovable? Try something gravity-stubborn, wind-ignoring, a testimonial your family can try to lift forever.

## Notes on a Poem I Wrote at Twelve

title suggestions: "Daddy Issues" or "Nomad Dad"

I'm in the shower saying goodbye to hairs curling around
my feet into silver holes. My heel holds a few strays
from wilting down the drain. They're still mine if I still see them.

These hairs remind me of eraser shavings I left
swirling around my notebook, cowering
at the sight of your apparitional name, Pops

*speaking around issue?*

*Is this really what the son wants?*

I'm avoiding the poem I started about you, father,
when bright vanilla clouds and morning birds   *Awkward*
roused my mind, reminding me of fathers with sons in parks.

*Mmm, smart word*

My trembling hand rhymed Dad with nomad. I tried
to erase what I started, wash my weary burdens
by ignoring you but words look like ghosts when you erase them.

I'm in the drain you let me fall down, writing poems
across the shadows you left, clogging these pipes  *whose pipes?*
you don't care to clean. I'm still yours when you don't see me.
*never*
                                                    *we get it...*

I prayed one day you'd read that poem where vanilla clouds
floated over lines where we share ice cream in evergreen
parks with a family of morning flycatchers that chirp over our laughs.

*Is Dad really a "stroll the park" kinda dude?*

Instead, you'll have to read this poem where I gather eraser shavings
like dead leaves, unfinished poems I was too scared to write
about you with imagery you were too cowardly to make with your son.

*Endnote on next page*

Matheus, ← my bad if that's misspelled

I'm seeing the "ownership" message throughout.
Poem has potential, but it feels like the son
is holding back.
Maybe just come out and say whatever you mean:
"Fuck you, Dad." or "Hey Dad, want to hang out"
or whatever...
Ever think you're being a tad dramatic?
Come on, you're around 12 by now.
You should be outside playing Spiderman.
Look, kid— sometimes things don't work out.
You're wanting to know what I'd think?
All I got is stop hiding behind
the metaphors, son.
I mean, you don't actually think I'll read
this stuff, do you? Me?
Do I strike you as the type of man
to give one shit about a poem?

52

**Which Batman Villain Is Your Deadbeat Dad?**

Quiz by Contributor *AccidentSon!*
[Results from User *BudLight_Daddy69*]
1. Choose a Catwoman:
    A. Anne Hathaway (The Dark Knight Rises)
    B. Zoë Kravitz (The Batman)
    C. *Not picky. But I'm partial to younger, vulnerable girls.*
    D. Michelle Pfeiffer (Batman Returns)
2. Pick a weapon of choice.
    A. Joker's Crowbar
    B. Mr. Freeze's Freeze Cannon
    C. Penguin's Machine Gun Umbrella
    D. *A little liquid courage goes a long way. You should see these kids' faces when I pull up with enough 6 packs to get everyone's beak wet.*
3. Think quick! The Caped Crusader has discovered Dad's secret lair. What's his move?
    A. Reveal the timebomb he's hidden under Gotham Harbor.
    B. *I've been to enough of these to smell when cops are coming. Some shithead geek snitches every time, and the pigs round here love to squeal about how many high school parties they've fucked up. But I believe in magic opportunities. There's this black girl that's so sloppy drunk she can't tell us what color her car is. I know, I know, chocolate is dangerous. I can keep it under wraps with my boys though. Wouldn't be nothing serious, nohow. Besides, who else is going to take this poor cutie home before the sirens bust us?*
    C. Surrender. It's all a part of the plan.
    D. Send in the goons!
4. Pick a Joker:
    A. Heath Ledger (The Dark Knight)
    B. Joaquin Phoenix (Joker)
    C. *Whichever one is damaged. But hell, I'm always up for a good joke. Even when they tell me something can't be funny, I'll slap my country charm on and have them laughing at cancer. Girls eat that shit up. Black Girl sure does. I get a little loose myself and—before you know it—we're at my Funhouse.*
    D. Zach Galifianakis (The LEGO Batman Movie)
5. Dad can't take down The World's Greatest Detective on his own. Who's his partner in crime?
    A. *Condoment King. Without a rubber, I'm desperate. So, I speak as sweetly as I can: "I'd hate to ruin the night. You sure, hun? I ran out of condoms,*

darlin, and I'm too drunk to go driving now. How about this..." I damn near seduce myself.
    B. Killer Moth
    C. Poison Ivy
    D. Polka-Dot Man
6. What's his tragic origin story?
    A. Fell in acid
    B. Lab accident cryogenically froze his lover
    C. Born a giant Man-Crocodile
    D. *You, boy. Never should've done it. It's not my place to tell a woman to get rid of a baby, but the bitch didn't tell me until she was six months along. I thought I could get away with it too, then you popped out white as paper. Still, I was hoping you weren't mine. Had the judge order a DNA test. Yup, you're mine, boy.*
7. The Bat fell right into Dad's trap! How would he dispatch the flying rodent?
    A. Before murder time, he takes Batman's cowl off in front of cameras. It's always fun to reveal a juicy secret.
    B. Why waste a perfectly good minion? Dad has always been proficient in mind control.
    C. *I've never been one for rats. Now I can't work for no company cause of child support; they'd just take it out of my check. I'll have to stay off grid—do a couple odd jobs so I don't lose every penny I make. Look, I don't mean any harm to you or your momma. But you were an accident, understand? I wasn't ready. Still ain't, to be honest. How about we cut a deal? You stay over there, and I'll stay over here. It's about keeping the peace. Isn't that right, little hero?*
    D. Keep it simple: one bullet, one cut throat, one punch through the gut, one back to break. Evil is best served simple. One ungraceful whack is enough to ruin a family forever.

Result:

**The bullet that killed Bruce Wayne's mother.** You're the beginning of the end. Quick, to-the-point, precise, irreversible, and everlasting. An ounce of silver cruelty for an unhealable scar.

**8 Comments**

PrincessStacy2354 – 30 minutes ago
    Hell yeah! I got Kite Man! Super underrated tbh.
SemiSibby – 2 weeks ago
    Bad quiz. Got killer croc, but am obviously joker. Also, where's the Heath Ledger respect?! Best joker hands down. Big RIP.

YoYoHalfBro – 1 month ago
    Does a bullet count as a villain?

[Hide reply]

    AccidentSon! – 1 month ago
        Hey bro, see you got the same result. Eh, it's
        close enough to a villain,
        I guess. It's an antagonistic force.

BlackMom19 – 2 years ago
    You need to delete this, sweetie.

[Hide replies]

    AccidentSon! – 2 years ago
        Which result did you get?

    BlackMom19 – 2 years ago
        It wasn't like this. We were both drunk.

    AccidentSon! – 2 years ago
        He was 30, Momma. He brought the beer.
        He knew what he was doing.

    BlackMom19 – 2 years ago
        Please take it down. It's best to leave the past in
        the past. All we can do is thank God that I got
        you out of all that. My Boy Wonder.

## Streaming Dreams Where Mom Didn't Have a Baby

### TV-MA| 58m |Stand-Up
Slapstick comedian poet sounds off on post-industrial feminism, hallucinations of his mom's life without him in the family pictures, and Taco Bell sauce packets during his fire-brand set using jokes and deflective forms to avoid deep-seated mental shit.

### TV-14| one season cut short |Because Momma had to drop out of college
At Tituba University, you must be willing to brew, broom, or rune your way to become the most powerful witch in East Texas. One Wiccan finds her future cursed and needs a little black magic to save her freshman year.

### TV-14| 1hr 34m |Documentary
Witness the untold fantasy of the child-free, sociocultural culinary icon, freedom fighter, Nobel-winning accountant, and world-renowned Mezzo-Soprano "Black Jane Goodall." Momma always said she would've been a vet.

### TV-MA| minutes adhered to your skull |Horror
28-year-old man craves brains and black flesh. High school girl just wants to taste her first beer. Hard to compromise with the undead, so why not beat some sense into them with a barbed-wire bat? Watch the girl escape being taken advantage of by an apocalypse man—escape carrying the child of a Bud Light-packing creep.

### PG| 1h 31m |#1 in Family
Love, laughter, leprechauns, and a life without having to ask your boy to pee in Aquafina bottles for drug tests. It's all a princess can ask for. Feather-touched is the head that wears the tiara.

### Parental Guidance Suggested| Plenty of time |Sci-Fi
Something is rotten, lying in state within a womb. Werner Herzog explores the effects 21 years of marinating in radioactive waste has had on one villager from Houston's Third Ward. Half-lyrebird, half-woman, sprouting tendrils of ambition, growing eyes of possibility on her shoulders.

### Indecent Language| 12m |Emmy-Nominated Limited Series
Ne Ne's eighteen-year-old daughter just returned from across the world with a cumbersome souvenir . . . a White man's baby. It's up to Granny to save her daughter from becoming my mom. She'll try a quick, convincing

whip of the tongue. Will her daughter listen? *Now's not the time. Whole life ahead of you.*
*Is this what you want?* Will Granny save herself the time of having to take the boy in twelve years after her daughter cuts an elbow on a concrete eviction notice?
It'll be a fucking hoot, I assure you.

**Therapist-approved| still figuring it out |Reality**
Blame and guilt corrode foundation rock off the spirit—carry her shards dream-long like the Caribbean wind carries sea salt. In this cerebral escapism, you are unburdened. An atmosphere of unpolluted fantasy. But the doctor says I shouldn't think this way. I'm media-washing my mind with airs and graces. Meth could have been an only child. Those men could have been worse if you weren't a mother. Maybe, the doctor tells me, I could have saved you. Your choices, I'm made to say. *Your choices.* But while watching these bleak-dappled screens, I can't help but dream of you binging on the life you traded for me.

**Optometry with Momma**

Okay, Ms. Perkins, this shouldn't take long. Tell me which seems clearer.

        1      or      2

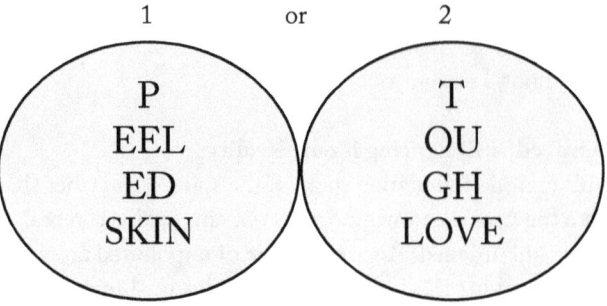

Interesting. How about these?

        1      or      2

**1.** Your boy was seven. He bundled half a dozen lightsabers around his body like a glowstick porcupine. From the neighborhood boys, he built a counsel. Galaxies were conquered, thumbs were bludgeoned, and the middle schoolers ran off with his sabers.

**2.** Your boy was spoiled rotten, an only child. A little forceful parenting never hurt anybody. Didn't hurt you. You didn't whip him much. Just enough to put the fear of God in him. That's what he needed. Those damn things were almost 20 apiece.

Hmm. Still no difference, huh? Give these a closer look:

        1      or      2

**1.** He cried home to Momma. Told all. You asked for his belt. You hacked his thighs for six minutes. *You should know better!* He babbled "Momma" through a mucusclotted throat. "Momma." You imagine it's a question. "Momma?" You chopped more youth off his bones.

**2.** Your lesson was a favor. You took your boy's legs away. Stung bones don't feel like ours anymore. Swish. With a little imagination, they became the middle school boys' legs. Swish, swish. And, for a moment, Swish. He had justice. Swish, swish. Balance.

Don't worry, ma'am. I have issues telling the differences myself.
Our eyes evolved to trick the soul—they blur, they decolor, they hallucinate. We say truth comes when we see it with our own eyes, but eyes did not evolve to see truth. They evolved for mothers to see alligator snouts while they bathed us in rivers. But now, what do you see, Momma?

     1      or      2

> A country where love doesn't come with an ass whoopin'. Where the Sith aren't running the show. A hippie-dippey, lovey-dovey, kiss-and-makeup paradise. Or maybe just a home of patience. A home of grace. Where sons never question who you are.

> A country with a breath of Anthrax, ready to whisper "hope" in your son's ear. The real world. The kill the black boy world. The beat that nigga till he screams for his momma world. The world that brands backs and snaps necks. Where pain is the vaccine for death.

Last one. I need you to help me see this, Momma. I need to know why we blur the line. What did you see? What lurks in the soul that makes a child's scream look identical to education?

    1    or    2

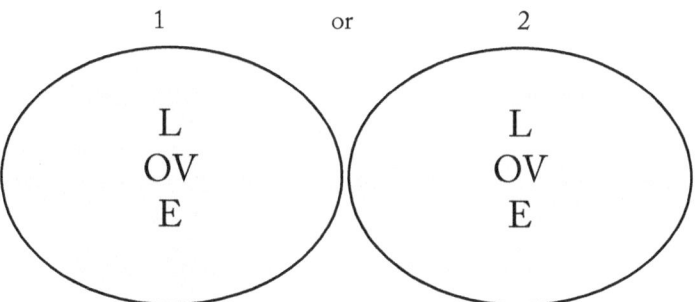

## The [            ] Dream Has a Baby in a Prison [           ]

Where's [            ] Momma   when [            ]
the soil [            ] grows arid

We wake [            ] each time we howl her name

The [            ] Dream   The [            ] Dream
[            ] left   this mother[            ]

Warden is [            ] scrapping [            ]
his   [            ] hungry tongue
A [            ] girl can't be [            ] more
Close [            ]

Momma rest your brain[            ]
Steal [            ] an American night[            ]

A sentence from [            ] our lives will be braided
by [            ] iron [            ]
Two juveniles [            ] in the [            ]yard
[            ]scotch[            ] on [            ] tongue

This [            ] Dream is too young   [            ]

Be [            ]ful of sacrifice Momma
These [            ]men will fillet [            ]our skin
and [            ] our [            ] spines [            ]
until our skeletons[ ] rust [            ]

**Footstool Sister**

My birthday was a crime scene. No one has their story straight.
> Momma says I was first out; I used my twin sister's face as a footstool, my gumdrop toes stretching toward life, inching sis's soft forehead toward an ovary, toward a deadly neck cord, noosing her, feticide before I could even open my eyes, discarding my mother's ability to have more little sisters.

This is not true, even though I believed it for ten years—and swore this is what Momma told me.
> Grandma says I never had a sister; Grandma was there when the fluorescent lights first singed my thin eyelids, saw the nurses' eyes pop through their masks and hairnets when they saw a bleak-white baby come out of a dark Black woman, held me—her daughter's only son—to the window so Auntie Lou could see me, hear Auntie Lou scream at the sight of me—well, more at the sight of "His Nuts! Oh Lord, what's wrong with his nuts! They're like acorns, poor baby!" They say my testicles were the only shade of black on me.

This is not true—at least it's not true anymore.
> Momma says they tried to have a natural birth but switched to a cesarean; my baby claws latched to her so deep they had to cut me out, the 39 hours of labor, oh the humanity, my desperate attempt to fight nature, to kill Macbeth, and—in all the excitement—I left a wound in her womb that will never heal.

Momma still references the scar. But I never latched onto anyone.
> Momma and Grandma later say that I was born asleep; too lazy to show up to my own birth awake, so serene they thought I was dead, "I don't hear him, I can't hear my baby," peace-infused, cheeks red with life's promises, "Dr. Nidson, what color is he?" They had to pinch my ass to wake me, everyone was *wahhh wahhhing* and *Thank Jesus*-ing.

I like the idea of this being true.
> Momma says they brought her the wrong baby; three babies graced the incubators that day, one Latin brown, one African American brown, and one confusedly White. They bring it sheathed in a cloak, like a hidden set up to a yo' momma joke, place it among the limp things my mother's hands had become, opened her the present, and she saw the Motherland hue, "Um. This isn't my son," *damn*, so close to going home with Mr. and Mrs. Martinez, did someone check the baby tag, must have been a typo. Who knows if

my incubator brothers made it to adulthood with the same story? Who's to say what's true anymore?

The key to a murder mystery is a red herring.

Auntie Shawn says I did have a sister, only not when I thought; she says that Momma was going to have a little girl after me, her name is an old sprite in her memory, not quite tangible but maybe it started with a J. I was two, she was a miscarriage. Auntie says Momma was so sick after she had me, playing footsie with death, scarred womb, never recovered, couldn't bear another child.

The other trick to a murder mystery is to suspect everyone.

I told myself the lie when I was five; there's a haze in memory, a virus that makes the unclear believable, that makes a five-year-old misconstrue his mother's attempt to explain why he doesn't have a sister into a thriller, where the scars he left when he was stretching into life did kill his sister, where he casts himself as the murderer in the tongue-in-cheek play.

Who would suspect the baby?

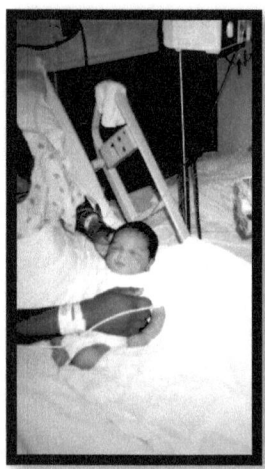

## Scene from the Reading

Lights on POET at a lectern: the hissing fly in a milk-walled room. Coughs and plastic bottle cracks snap in the air like applause. MOMMA stands in the audience; her happy cheeks are held so high that it makes her face look like a heart. She will never sit down; she's extended the stage to her feet.

### POET

(ruffling with the loose leaf *The Grace of Black Mothers* manuscript) Hello, everyone. This first poem is about my mother and me growing up poor in Houston. (Leans into the silence as eager to ignite as a blunt's tip. Then, past the silence all the way to break down the glassy doors of Momma's eyes. *Did you notice I said we were growing up?* his eyes tell her) Momma, we were rats in Houston.

> *POET lets it out: their tattered soles on Houston's hot pavement, eviction notices mangling their lives, the here-and-there, stop-and-start, pack-and-unpack, get-and-give, run-and-stop, home-and-homeless, bruise-and-breathe, living-and-dying, safe-and-stowaway life she tethered them to. He had written it like she'd been dead, like she would never hear it. Another lie to make the truth pronounceable. He kept going. He called his father his rightful name: a predator. He unhid the grief that family album smiles had buried. He tried to be Black, to be a son, to be saved. He inhales the air of tension and speaks the final line.*

### POET

You put us there, Momma. And it hurt. All of it. (finishing) Thank you.

### MOMMA

(clapping in the audience, an ovation she was already standing for) That's my boy. I love you, sweetie. That's my boy! (in a whisper to herself) It's only for the art. It's only for the art.

*It's a dark room. The only sound is her claps, her proud, frantic claps. This was what it was all for. Mom sacrifices her life for her son. She's a good mom.*

She's a good mom.

**Scholarship Letter**

Dear Money,

    Where art thou, O green-eyed monster? Joking. I thought you'd appreciate a highbrow Shakespeare reference. Of course, the only time your brows get high is when families that look like ours come in to ask for small business loans. Bango! Kidding, of course, you know we love you. Seriously how are the kids? Still don't understand this crypto business.

    Anywho, I'm contacting to say thank you. I think we're finally starting to understand one another. You know, my mother always told me to keep my eye on the—well you. And I'm glad I did. Speaking of Momma, I'll admit she's the other reason I'm writing. You know I hate to do this, but can you send a teensy-weensy spot of green luck her way? She just doesn't understand you like I do. And well, once you get in a pit, it's hard to dig out. But she has potential, I swear. She's the one who taught me White Voice, remember! "Talk like a Disney boy when you're with your teachers, baby," she'd say, peanutbuttering my sandwiches. "*Talk. Like. This.* And them teachers will just love you." She's a natural. She skates between AAVE and your language like an Amtrak. But we both know that's not enough.

    Those "Accommodating Your Peers: An Angry Black Woman's Guide to Being Less Angry, Black, and Womanly" training videos you sent through her employer's mouths haven't worked, even though she *really, really* adores them. The problem rests with something deeper. She's been beaten down to soot. It's in her nature to sacrifice herself. Even though we've been separated for eight years, she still looks in the mirror to see a commodity.

    She's been asking me for 20s for the past four months. She'll get on her feet eventually, I know it. But maybe a little push wouldn't hurt? Anyway, don't be a stranger or I'll be in serious financial danger.

As sincere as I can be,
- An indebted son

## Aiyana Mo'Nay Stanley-Jones Picks a College Major

princesses lose their outlines in the dark    blurred shouts
    Crayola menagerie    crumbs of color beneath a fingernail
hairclip    plastic flowers    hair-clipped plastic dandelion wind fever
Herbology        Botany
ruffled frog pajamas    small body quilt—folded at the edge of the tent
English    and Dead Sea language to decipher howls—that air-grasping
straws burning on the edge of a Saturn-pulled vision
    *You know I never touched you, Officer Weekly*
braids slug cold and a toppled tiara
    *they came in and killed my baby*
U.S. History    Politics    Film and Television
reality bends and hooks in the corners of firelight—
breathe teargas until you can't
a sister a mother a niece a daughter a grandmother a
    Little Tikes coupe was in the front yard    Military Science
incalculable casualties    lose count    Mathematics    lose motion    Physics
how heavy is a seven-year-old with a hole in her head?    ounce of silver
something to rip apart the dream of what    of    Communications

  Juniper-eyed solstice berry,
        you see    how easily one hides behind words?
Poetry    something to slip between the strokes
on a canvas    something
hang-holed    greased in gasoline    flame    Dance
  because what more can be said?
eat the graffitied poem in your textbooks    squeeze your tongues dry
*I gets no sleep*    *the flashbacks*
*I wouldn't wish them on nobody in the world*
*not even you, Officer*
princesses will learn to waltz    will learn to queen.

**They Were Killed Holding**

a garden hoe,
a toy,
a bad check,
a cell phone,
a bag of Skittles,
a life alert button
a White girl's hand,
keys to their own apartment, CDs, an oven mitt,
loose cigarettes, steering wheels, their last blunt—
holding nothing at all.
Holding their tongues—holding their breaths—holding
their hands to the starless air—holding cement in their teeth—holding
their bullet-chewed arteries—holding promises to come home—holding
Momma's name in their stomped throats—holding

Granny's love handles
as they fell asleep
watching cartoons.

### Mamie Till-Mobley's Reddit Post

### AITA for Showing My Son's Battered Face to the Media So America Could See What They Did to My Baby?
[*Pinned by Moderators of* r/AmItheAsshole]
Posted by u/Mamie_Till 2 months ago

Like everyone I know, I read Jet Magazine. It always has pretty women on the cover looking for something better to do than grin in their brassieres. I thought to write to John Johnson about having a photographer come down for Emmett's funeral. I got tired of people looking away from my son. Those men, that jury, that courthouse, that country made him look like a thing. It's easy to look past things.

I thought the pictures would make it mean something.

Am I the asshole? America had to see his face. What was I supposed to do? Those men stomped my son into mud and left him to rot. I couldn't just let my baby be gone like that. I know I did the right thing. Then, I got letters. Thank yous and death threats. More thank yous, and then I started speaking more and I hated it. I hated that I needed to do it.

Am I the asshole? I can't be, can I? We started something. My boy was able to show this country what will happen if we don't change. I know I did right by my baby.

But it still feels like cockroaches are crawling around my heart. It still feels like there's a part of me that wants to kill somebody. I know I shouldn't, and I wouldn't. But I keep feeling eyes that won't look away.

All I wanted was to have a son. Help him pick out his ties and make cornbread the way he liked it. What am I now? A spokesperson? What do I have? Pictures of a thing that used to be my boy?

Am I the asshole? For making you look.

No. If I could look, you could look. Let's face it, you need to see him. I've been dead 20 years and you're still killing Emmetts.

Maybe y'all need us to be assholes.
Maybe y'all need howls to curdle in your veins.

**All the Black Mothers in America Hold a Press Conference**

Are you getting our good sides? Enough
lighting for our spilled ebony shadows?

We martyrized carolers singing
for our body bag boys and girls.

Here we are again, with Ben Crump
and Al Sharpton's hands on our shoulders

smogged by their sweat, Black Opium cologne,
and the grey-lipped slogans they first preached

17,000 dead sons ago. We're learning
rehearsed hope, buzzkill words, the art

of pretending. That's the game, right?
We feed tears to snaky mic cords

and you soundbite us—chop our dead
babies into segments before sports breaks.

Then, we pretend to be calm, to be
prepared for this, and you pretend to—

Wait, don't go! Did we mention his favorite
basketball player was James Harden, ABC13?

And Fox26, here's a crayon sketch of her future
(pre-lynching). We can hold it for B-roll?

What's wrong, KHOU-Local? Boys shot
into pulp can't compete with Bigfoot sightings?

Any questions about how we saved grace? How
we painted tender black songs between the stars?

## The [American] Dream Has a Baby in a Prison [Hospital]

Where's [America's] Momma   when [we need her]
the soil [in her throat] grows arid

We wake [her corpse]     each time we howl her name

The [American] Dream    The [American] Dream
[we never] left  this mother['s dream]

Warden is [here] scrapping [barnacles off]
his   [kiss] hungry tongue
A [little Black] girl can't be [little no] more
Close [the cells]

Momma rest your brain[stem on a]
Steal [bench and block out] an American night[mare]

A sentence from [now]     our lives will be braided
by [blunt] iron [bars]
Two juveniles [jumping rope]   in the [court]yard
[hop]scotch[ing] on [America's] tongue

This [American] Dream is too young      [for Death Row]

Be [care]ful of sacrifice Momma
These [country]men will fillet [y]our skin
and [fuse] our [torn] spines [together]
until our skeletons['] rust [flutters away]

**my**

# Thea,

you left town cavity-hearted sweetie sweetie
packed sweet decaying promises in a drawstring bag.
Left a boy to be raised solely beneath the sweetie
sweetie burn bark trees of his Granny's house. sweetie sweetie sweetie
sweetie sweetie
sweetie Thea, the sweetie dancer, the Shelby County Sweetheart
sweetie loved that son as much as a stillborn loves a daydream sweetie
sweetie sweetie sweetie sweetie sweetie
watching Zoro, you told him *I can't take you back,* sweetie, sweetie sweetie
*if you stay with me on the streets, you'll end up*

*just promise me you'll stay in school—make enough money for both of us.*
*Buy your Momma an MTV crib one day.*

Thea, that sweetie boy promises
to bolt across concrete cracks of sidewalk
lightning to keep
from stumbling down them
    like you
        did
                for him

That boy loves you—
but needed time to trace his courage toward

# Act III

# Saving Grace

*My baby, forgive these hands for all they let slip.*

## Southern Hymns

Before this nostalgia expires,
I want to talk about sunset
cicada songs peeling paint off
our tin trailer, and all those curses—
badass as they were.

My personal favorite threat was,
"Watch ya mouth or I'll slap the taste out of it,"
spoken under a warm, pink afternoon.
And who could forget that wonderful ditty,
"Your ass is grass," harmonizing with
recline chair creaks and orange cap-gun pops.

It's all so romantic—so sentimental:
sniffing dry pine, chasing mint green
lizards, "I brought you into this world
I can take you out," St. Augustine grass
between brown toes, fresh cans of whoop-
ass served with cornbread and greens—
mmm, home.

Take me back, where brutal tongues
fan away brow sweat on those
balmy Southern days—
where we dipped our love in violence
and passed it down like hymns.

# FATALITY!

*after kicking my auntie's ass in a fighting game*

| SPECIAL MOVES | INPUT COMMAND | DAMAGE | BLOCK TYPE |
|---|---|---|---|
| Dashiki Shoryuken | ←, ←, ⊗ | 50 [+ on block] | mid |
| 10x gal Coconut Oil Jar Combo | (midair, rains down) →, ↘, ◎ *keep laughing and you'll stay ashy, white boy* | 88 [poison effect] | too buttery; made to slip through defenses |
| Auntie Shawn's signature Hurricane Katrina Kick or Kaepernick Tiger Knee | ↑, →, + ◉ (alt move with) ® | insta kill [Black and grey Panther ready to laugh within the dumpster fireball] | high expectations |
| Get Over Here! Unblockable Chain Grab Hug | ←, ↙, ↑, →, ↓, ↵, ↝, ↓, ↻, →, ↘, ↪, ↗, ↙, ⸸, ⇊, ←, ⁉, ⚔, ↖, ↘ | 0 (avoidant taunt) | Your nephew never quite finds the words to say he loves you. |
| Spamming *white boy* when I talked about Minecraft and debate practice; *little nigga* when I marinated two thighs and a drum in mashed potatoes, called it *Sharktankable* | (while being reminded of my talented tenth, light-skinned privileges) ⇊, ∆, →, ↗ | 10 [projectile projection— the reason I'm always thinking about race] | low blow but deserved. Taught me the funniest way to bare teeth when they sear my bones |
| Invisibility | Ne Ne's/your mother's pea tumor ↗↗ into walnut, ⊗, ♥, Momma/your sister ↕ in ®ehab | internal [I'm just glad we had each other] | never knew you offered to adopt me while Momma got her footing |

We were in the room when Ne Ne had her stroke, shared her frustration about *a man trapped inside her Facebook*, her nerves sizzling, taut neck like a fishhook strung by the ceiling. I never told you how that memory tightens—belts my skin. We never talked about how to fight with grace. Read to me Assata Shakur again. Before I pass the four cheese potatoes, once more, smack me with Fannie Lou Hamer. Ella Baker can be our mother for an evening of button mashing.

| You read my first poem | (when I'm 12 years old) George Stinney finds my tongue → they ran his mother out of town before ◎ + \ alone for his own execution ⊗ ↗ too tiny for the straps ⊕ Bible booster seat ←, ←, old sparky →, ⊕ | *George Stinney was 14, and they killed him anyway. He joined the search party to find those little White girls, and they killed him anyway* | low as rootwood—but you said *keep going.* |
|---|---|---|---|

grief leaves a soul in tar ↑ we take a breath drag ↑ mud through our stomach say *fighter* ↑ say *fire* ↑ tender as a memory's last hour ↑ break *their jaws* you said ↑ *don't be a punk* you demand ↑ but I wish this was over ↑ they won't stop killing us won't stop cheating us ↑ this dream ↑ you're the last person alive who heard your little sister have a dream for when <u>she</u> grows up ↑ you beg me to shred the walls of a dream-drying system ↑ but auntie ↑ they won't stop hurting her ↑ Momma loves me but she can't find grace ↑ if I scrape tar from my stomach what will I do with the scars it leaves ↑ across town my white friend just unwrapped a ps5 ↑ can I play ↑ maybe I'll beat him ↑ at his own game

**The Welfare Queen Pyrate Code**

1. Every Black woman has a vote in the affairs of Black bounty; has equal title to the freshest provisions, strongest Patrón and Crown Royal Apple. If liquors be made scarce by port authorities, or the government limits itself in the crew's direction, seize they shit. Shiver our chicken tenders, king crab legs, and on-brand cereal out their pockets.

2. Every Black woman will be SNAP-enrolled fairly when it's her turn to be Treasure's succubus. On these occasions, be a bougie bitch: ebony Frances Grey brim, 24-karat nameplate, Versace Couture Deluxe Tuberose perfume, Shy Diva coat.
If congressmen defraud the company of dollas, jewels, or gold caps for our babes' teeth—if they declare poverty must come with a uniform—maroon their pasty asses. Remember their original robbery and set them betwixt a debt-rippled shore and ass-whoopin'.

3. At nautical twilight, lights, candles, and bouquets will try to be put out by police curfew; stay vigil-weary for our drowned girls and boys.

4. Keep voice, pistol, and cutlass clean for service.

5. To avoid scurvy, sip from moonrock, spit out star-steamed tobacco plucked from a decaying orchard of deferred dreams and dead bodies. We're still splintered by the slaver's shipboards.

6. To desert our just deserts—to blockade our baby boatswains from a well-deserved dessert will be discouraged.

7. No pryate will quarrel with their own stamped skin. No special favours from the Quartermaster.
    We all starboard niggas.
That means you well-to-do colony hoes can shut the fuck up if you don't partake in the code. That means brown pyrates, beige pyrates, Indigenous pyrates, rural pyrates, trans pyrates, pyrates with disabilities, gay pyrates, and immigrant pyrates won't taste the smoketail of a Black flag's cannonball.

8. Hymn weavers have rest on Sabbath Day.
Make suffering a remnant of the sea salt breeze.
It's much work believing our souls weigh more in gold
while they're being devoted to others' lives.

9. To keep our bodies nerve-chill. They want to see rowdy niggas. They want to see doubloon goons begging for Captain Crunch and Milky Ways. They want to steal our right to own our rites. They want us to wrap bootstraps around our peg legs. They want a "big booty, hooped-earring bitch" to stand silent
as their spit drips down her forehead.
        So cut out their spitting tongue and make it a necklace.
        We walked their plank plenty. Plunder away.
        Plunder till we get paid.

**Dear Swiss Rolls**

       It's been so long since we've seen each other. I see you've moved up a couple shelves, no longer slinking at the bottom with your Nutty Buddies. Can I ask a favor? I need to eat you, here—in this Kroger—with these chill snaps being sent over from the round packages of ground beef and turkey. I mean no harm by it; I've just missed you. Other shoppers are starting to stare at us, so I'll try to make this quick.

       When's the last time we were all together? How long ago were my legs crossed between the bars of a shopping cart pushed by my Ne Ne— her pearls bright under these grocery store lights. We came after church to see you. One time, she let me open your box in the cart. I rolled around like a marble, giggling as she turned corners like a NASCAR driver. You don't understand how much I've missed this: seeing your two chocolate logs sitting in mountain snow as white as your cream swirls. Remember when we ate the strips of chocolate you left on the white cards slid beneath you? We were never wasteful.

       *Where is she?* Well, she can't be here. She's gone—that's why I need your help. I was hoping that you would bring me back to her. Look, I have a cart and it's Sunday, just like old times. You came in pairs, and we'd share you in the living room while watching Vanna White's sequins sparkle from Es to Ls. I was hoping that when I tasted your roulade icing, I could remember more details about her. Maybe, I would even see her hands—her fingers wrapped in church jewelry—gripped on the shopping cart one more time. Age has made me forget the finer details of her hands, her wrinkled cheeks rising when she smiled. You must miss that smile, too; the one she gave after saying, "We can't eat the whole box, sweet tooth."

       It would mean the world to me to taste those memories. Those chocolate sweet moments when she handed me her Swiss Roll because I was finished with mine.

**Ode to Toaster Ovens**

Someone told me Odes must match
   their zombie subjects in beauty.
So, when we finish here, this poem
   will be balled up and hidden.
This poem will lose itself in nostalgia,
   nudge its way around history.
It'll bump into shit, knock-over vases.
   It'll try to dance with its bad leg.
It'll sit at a bench and think,
   "Here. Here is where I met her smile."
This poem will rummage and wade
   through its grandma's boxes
and find itself in black and white
   remember its childhood nickname:
"Ode. Oh, how could I forget? I'm
   an ode. My ink is the last breath.
I come too late. I devour silence."
   And this ode will see its end.
It'll lean into your ear and ask,
   "Won't you remember toaster ovens?
Won't you remember your Mammy's
   casserole dish her mammy gave her?
Won't you remember that ugly
   ass prom dress your auntie wore?
Uncle's MASH DVDs, the stuffed bears
   you mauled, the wine stains
from the fights, your backyard tree.
   Don't blow me away like
the dust on Granny's crock pot."

**Grace Must Be**

An aging mother:
her tender brown knuckles
to my boiling forehead,
her Tootsie Roll voice
bouncing over midnight
stories as she ignores
my weight on
her aching knee.
  When she floats away,
  does Grace leave too?
Can I find it in lamplight
lying on midnight poems,
cupping grey words
in bright hands?
Can we lose Grace
when an honest
lineage is a burden?

Maybe Grace is folding poem pages
into paper boats to float after them.
Odes inked onto manilla hulls,
soaking brine, sinking into murky water.
  Forgiveness, her old hand
  pointing through me.

**Dominoes**

Is it wrong that I daydream about reviving my grandmother to school her at a game of dominoes? And I mean embarrass her—make her wish our continent never discovered dominos. Before you pearl-clutch, you should know that the last time we played, she gave me her final domino and told me to choose how I wanted to go out.
Then she said, "We call that an ass-whooping, Junior."
All I want is a few more eternities to pay her back, then play again.

## Church Jewelry and Mourning Dead Words
*from Ne Ne's Journal*

November 2017

*The weather is cool - now*. I want to believe
these days of sweating my ass off are long dead.
Sitting here, I feel as young as *Mar*. Writing these words
reminds me of a baby girl diary I wrote in every morning.
Before *I had a stroke*, I wore age like costume jewelry:
a sapphire pendant to slip off after church.

Now, age wears me— *strings* to my *Limbs*. Hard to believe
I was ever a young thing! But I was, damnit. Good hair, jewelry,
*Pants Dresses Blouses*. Since *surgery on 13th of Nov* I've slept like the dead—
After I heal my mind, I'll get time to feel beautiful. Next morning,
*Martheaus* is helping me with my *Rehab* words.

January 2018

*The My team won*. So, *I had a good morning*
Silence tastes like *Okra*. A tumor traps my words, but I believe
healing is hearing second hands *hsk*, cicadas hymning. If I'm dead
by *February, Shawn* will buy me Air Jordans and onyx jewelry.

I stare speechless as *Mar* mouths for both of us—speaking like I'm dead.
I'd like to learn *how to take my pill my self*. But in silence, I hear relief
Death is on the porch rocking chair. I *May go home* tomorrow morning.

My soul's tender. The only " *Medicine* " I've got left requires belief.
I'll *Drink and Be Happy* because *Thoday* I am not dead.

All I need is *Roses and your gal well. I will keep* believing!

March 2018

*Thore in the head* they took my top
of my head off. words, *Not* return.
jewels to me- *Leaving*

April 2018

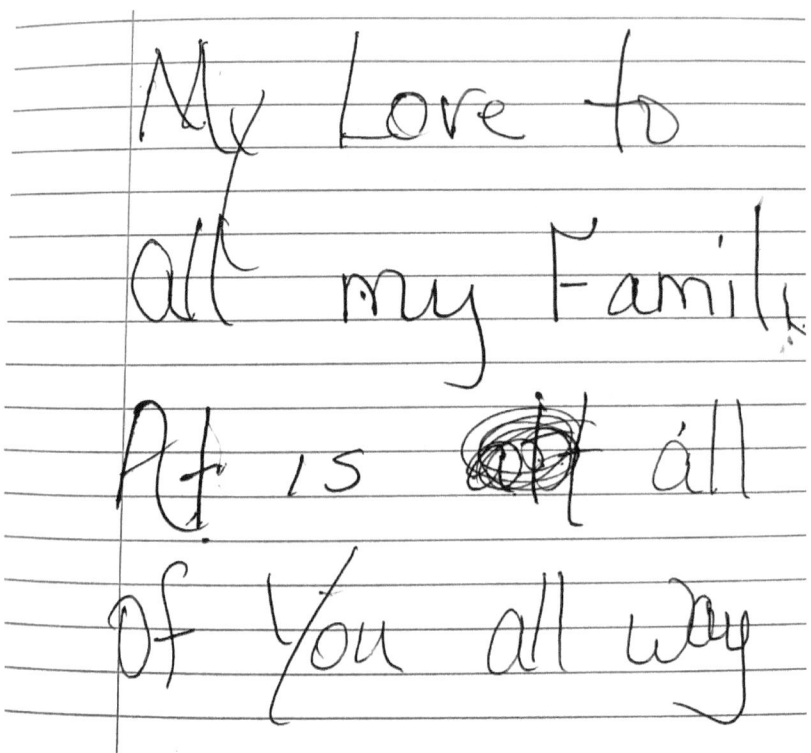

My Love to all my Family. At is ~~of~~ all of You all way

**Mothers Singing Their Souls Out**
    *for Nina, Billie, Mahalia, Etta, Ella, and Aretha*

We're in a Harlem bar, ceilings cigar-stained,
    the night is drunk on power, darkening
        till opium, till the only thing we see is fire
            kindling from their throats—can you hear 'em, boys?
    Mothers of a Black Revolution making the whole house quiver.
    Let your feet shuffle    on your way    to Canaan Land.
      Sway dirty, you strange fruits,      you spellbound boys.
           Run, sinnermen!      Run dogs—

    This hell-tongue tenor gotcha feeling good!
      Rock steady      jump to it      say a little prayer
        'cause our misery can't stop stomping its foot
      through the planked dance floor of History.

Mommas, take us home—we Black kids are tipsy on your fever pitch,
our heart-burdened chests following the tempo of your North Star songs.

**Amazing Grace**

As a boy, I thought "Amazing Grace" was the National Anthem for Black people. I had only ever heard it sung by Black women—lullabying us with high octaves and belted whispers.

When Miss Marleen, in her daisy dress, pulled out Mary Hoffman's book, I thought she was only reading to me—to the Black boys and Black girls.

Grace looked just like Momma. Grace was young. Grace was pigtails and gap-toothed smiles.
For years, I sing the lyric as
    *Amazing Grace,      how sweet         the sun.*
because I knew the sun gave Momma her dark skin
and I knew Black meant sweet.
        *That saved a wench     like me.*
wench became *Black mother*.
I didn't know what it meant, or even that it wasn't
the right word. Its meaning became *stubborn dreamer*.
        *I once was lost       but now I'm free.*
Grace must be the kindergarten mat, my square
with the daisy-bright star, and Miss Marleen
correcting my lyrics with damp eyes.

**Beyoncé, a Black Man Wants to Tell You**

He's a diva dappling this planet's surface with all the single ladies—
that he too gets in formation to make dancefloors
from kitchen linoleum and porch planks.
This evening, he'll fuck up the night with you,
cooing his neighbors awake.

Queen B, everything this Black man knows about sexiness
was inherited from your "Drunk in Love" music video.
He'll be all night bellowing that Anubis-infused track,
quenching his thirst with beach water,
hollering for a love to get drunk on.

Bey, a Black man wants to tell you none of his lovers
have ever seen him dance. He won't give himself
the freedom—freedom to throw it back
because he hates the way he moves.

But let this night flicker flawless; let's become an American problem.
He's tired of dashing his halo light like a candle in a hurricane.
Tonight, he'll surfboard to grace with all
Black men, Black folk, Black mothers.

Miss Third Ward, a 10-year-old H-town boy needs to thank you
for giving his momma a dollop of bliss before the morning sun
scorched her secret life—for letting her carve a tune:
a moment alone, a silent sip of lemonade before tucking us in,
wash-ragging our pearly skin, unknotting our nappy braids—
for loving her.

Tonight, he knows why hearing your voice crumple and tear
on "Pretty Hurts" made his Black mother cry downstairs.
She thought she was alone.

When I was a boy, I did not understand,
but if this Black man could go back, he'd say,
*You're pretty, Momma. Our face is allowed to be pretty.*

**Back When We Danced**

There's a Nile-long legacy of this family
  hitting boogies in deep East Texas dancehalls
high as Cooter Brown, night sky coal caught
    in our coughing throats.
Ne Ne's smile staining sepia evenings white.
I see her loose-strung fingers twisting curls
    on a soul ballad's tender head.
*Listen up*, she tells a Betty Wright song, *Imma show you proof
music was invented by a woman.*
     Eventually, these bonnet-capped nighttimes brought
three daughters, brought meat to bones, shivers to songs—
and as we do—she smothered her legacies in hand-me-down fortunes.
    My eldest auntie had Ne Ne's knees forecasting Lydian sunrises;
second auntie shed strings of notes from Ne Ne's bird blues.
She wanted her babies to steal her groove—
    and here comes Momma: heartbeat jazz since she was a little one,
the Chaparral captain, the dance team cheetah pirouetting across
a marching band summer's stubborn drums.
    She could've danced in college if—    Damn
Momma looks happy.
And damn, Ne Ne looks proud. Before I got there—
    "Graced" them with age. Back when they used to dance.
Time has taught me Blues
was a misnomer. We've been singing Blue Nile
  blues, bluebonnets blooming blues, bluebirds soaring
blues. The base of a flame's tongue blues.
  Revolutionary tempos are rising, Black keys are lit;
each blue beetle wants to jump in this pocket.
Grief, guilt. Every diminished dream-chord
   that came with this baby boy blue—
                        I'm ready to let it go.
Arpeggio, arpeggio. Let our saxophone blow.

## A Dream's Child

A ▮▮▮ mother has a baby—                        [Black]
▮▮▮▮▮ herself.                                   [is a baby]
She's a ▮▮▮▮▮ daydreamer                         [shackled]
who got pierced
▮▮▮▮▮▮▮▮▮▮▮▮▮▮▮▮▮▮▮           [by the burden living in her womb]
by a sudden water break
in her com▮▮▮▮▮ college cafeteria line.          [mutiny]

Maybe we mold children
out of the American Dream
from the ▮▮▮▮▮ crimson                           [shredded]
strips of our flag
and paint a ▮▮▮▮▮ fantasy                        [gnashed]
on a ▮▮▮ young mother's brain                    [too]
in▮▮▮▮▮ hopes that she'll weave                  [carcerated]
our country's ▮▮▮▮▮ threads.                     [White]

A Dream's spine can be as frail
as a petal ▮▮▮▮▮▮▮▮▮▮▮                           [split from its roots]
when weighed down
by a ▮▮▮▮▮ loaded gut                            [burden-]
nobody wants ▮▮▮▮▮ anymore.                      [this child]

**Three Black Sons, Three Black Mothers**

| | |
|---|---|
| George Stinney, Who Killed Two Little Girls, Dies | Howl, mommas . . . |
| Calmly . . . fourteen-year-old negro boy . . . | Scream . . . incoherent |
| youngest ever executed | Scream . . . your boys' names . . . |
| within South Carolina . . . | Aime . . . scream . . . for George |
| Bible under his arm . . . | your scrawny, smiling boy . . . |
| Guards had difficulty | with a . . . persimmon . . . breath |
| strapping the boy's slight | on his way to join the search . . . |
| forth into position in | Inhale his scorched . . . skin . . . from the sky . . . |
| the wooden chair . . . | Before . . . you blame yourself . . . for leaving . . . |
| no comment. | croon to guilt . . . that crooked nowhere we built . . . |
| | |
| White gang chases black to his death . . . white thugs | Weep, . . . Miss Jean, |
| wielding baseball bats . . . bruised body found | speak . . . for Brooklyn |
| at 1:03 a.m . . . ."Come here, | Harmonize . . . with . . . |
| nigger, come here . . . nigger . . . There's | Harlem mommas . . . then . . . |
| niggers in the pizza | Houston . . . Memphis . . . Sanford |
| parlor. Let's go kill em, | L.A . . . Baltimore . . . Weep . . . |
| boys" . . . A mother weeps | about . . . Michael's construction |
| in Brooklyn . . . "He said | job . . . building up . . . Here's a picture . . . |
| we would all | how handsome . . . Why—why my boy? Show us . . . |
| be happy!" | creep . . . into the stories . . . like coal dust . . . |
| | |
| Video shows Tyre Nichols calling for | Miss Nichols . . . |
| mother . . . beaten by officers | cut . . . caution tape |
| now charged in his death . . . video | . . . be scared . . . but keep |
| released by city . . . medics | howling . . . Tyre . . . They |
| arrive minutes after | thrive . . . when hymns . . . are whispered |
| officers disengage . . . | . . . Hold your weight . . . still . . . on the |
| left on the pavement | front porch . . . six-hundred and ten |
| . . . a traffic stop . . . | baby steps away, your son dies . . . |
| "I'm just trying | a familiar . . . shade . . . He wails for you . . . |
| to go home." | Holler back . . . howl your tongue dry . . . reach him . . . Try. |

**After Visiting Jasper, Texas**

Many versions of this document tried to be nonfiction—
tried to include the details of that 1998 evening.
Metaphor the chain, reclaim the pick-up truck.
Make it pretty-worded; make it new.

But my fingers are too weak to keep telling of a man's skin
grating off on an East Texas backroad.
I'll save kindling those more gruesome details
from the pyre of a White page.

Instead, while I hold myself awake,
I'd like to try showing a mother.
His mother.

Six years after her son's lynching, Stella Byrd scrapes her knee
scrubbing "Dead Nigger" graffiti off her boy's toppled gravestone.
She's 79.

As her cut scabs, she will meet a governor, wail for reform, create
a foundation in her son's name. As she and her nieces
brush pine needles and boot scruff off James' plot, she will bite down
on the bones of an old hymn: keep it from fluttering away. She will pray—
for many many hours—for those body desecrators.

It would be a lie to tell you I believe in prayer. But I swear to this:
daylight faded into the breeze hours ago. I have paced this graveyard,
staring at Ms. Byrd's stone, staring at James Byrd Jr's name,
counting abandoned petalskins, waiting for a song.

All while a bluebird—as sweet as our state's bonnets—has peered down,
perched from a god's shoulder. Weary, curious, I cannot say.
And as far as truth goes, she is all my spirit can cradle tonight.

**my**

us,

where there is too much noise
to give a Black mother grace.
We babies would howl our soundless hymns,
but only God has the instruments to create silence.   God             God
if you won't save us babies                    at least save our mothers
     America          America
Our family cookout has been ransacked of her babies baby baby baby baby
We grew up with Death's spit strolling down our eyelids baby baby baby baby
babies shot baby baby up the street baby babies hungry baby baby baby baby baby
babies milk-fed sour        music, TV, internet baby baby baby baby baby
nowhere a baby can go

America
and     his cradle-
song   promises
will     only ever be
the weight    of a dream
     for     us    babies
Too    many   anthems
    not     enough moments of    silence.
Tell Us, do you think we can make a silence as black as what opens
in a child's sweetheart when he's told *there are no more homes with roofs
for you and me to live unspoiled?* Tell Us, do you think we can make a silence
as black as what Sonya Massey will tell her children once they graduate? A shush.

     Shush.                              Shush.

# An American Dream's Night Stroll
   *for Ahmaud Arbery*

with a blunt (a two-hander) plucked from a concrete rosebush. The Dream is in the wrong neighborhood. Backyard gardens with chicken wire fence: inky hands crisscrossed to keep miracle fruits from piercing fingernails. A spring drop forest spoons the neighborhood, its Black Locusts branch out like filleted sinew. Within the cul-de-sac city, trees impress their dying: cigarette buds shaped into bottled lightning: white bark with dark scars. The Dream is alone with a black-skinned night. June bugs scrape The Dream's knuckles and laugh. Shoelaces *hiss* and slither in shadow pools. The blunt and hoodie keep The Dream's chest warmloved. Wormwood boards creak like keys from the boxy houses. The Dream is alone with a black-skinned night. Until. Truck lights. Chill snaps surf through The Dream's frizzy hair. The sidewalk is drowned-silent from The Dream's heaving sprint. Rounding the corner, The Dream stows away in a construction site. The Dream is alone with a black-skinned night. The Dream's lips singe on the blunt's promise. *Satilla River*, it thinks, *will rinse me*. Twelve blood beetles lindy hop on The Dream's throat cords; bliss bleeds its eyes. Until. Truck lights. The Dream takes off its Nikes to run. Until. Shotgun.

Truck lights whiten the neighborhood with sour smoke: tumbleweed-twirling between the unbuilt tracks of sky. The Dream winks dust on a black-skinned night. Until. Graveyard beetles rattle the block: erode the roads with needle-sharp legs. They sing an insect song: baritone and countertenor. The beetles scuttle-rush and swallow the truck lights. The beetles singin', *Where's the damn Devil? I want a damn deal. Where's Sneaky Satan? My souls sittin' still.* The Dream feels its organs separate like gas atoms; millions of armored husks wave-wash The Dream's body. Until. A mouth of okra and grits: the sound of a new basketball pinching rust of an elementary school hoop: Cadillacs sailing on ash: whisper-thin soul-jazz dripping over America like caramel on apples: tambourine howls, cornbread. The Dream inhales a black-skinned night.

**The Grace of Black Mothers**

Grace is the Dream that won't wake up.
   A magnolia tree to slumber under.
Grace is a choice, a gift, a nappy-haired baby on Saturday morning.
Grace is a grandson leaf-blowing his grandma's rocky grave
   on Thanksgiving.
Grace is a lie load-bearers use to Cha-Cha slide and boogie-woogie.
Grace is pine air and apple fritters with the tiniest hint
   of musk and grass.
Grace is the back that can carry any weight—an untippable scale.
Grace is sterling silver hymns, glimmers our people pass down.
Grace is forgiveness, it's kicking grief in the gut and getting ready
   to get kicked back.
Grace is a delicacy. It's a Smokey Robinson, Whitney Houston
   kind of tune.
Grace comes with wings—look up to see its bird droplets hit your
   forehead.
Grace is a Swiss Roll, a domino table, a story we keep
   because we can't keep each other.
Grace is a single Black mother teaching History how to dance,
   tired as hell, no sign of stopping.
   Inexhaustible. Unburdened.

**Center, Texas**

Ne Ne rescued me from Momma and Houston
after learning we were homeless.
Her piney woods trailer is wig spray, sandalwood, and stability.
                                                    I love it there.

One afternoon, a stench like an army of musty, dead dogs invades
her kitchen's air. The bloated belly of her pantry sags—calls
fungal songs, rattles decay.
We clean flea market cutlery for hours, sniff through
a hoarder's delight of paint-chipped pots. Until
a murky flower vase: maggot-soaked,
and a furry black lump like a suspended tumor.

The four horsemen of funky shit raid our nostrils
*Rotten shit,* Ne Ne spits. Smells like aftermath
of a Viking horde—men leave their stink.

A rat, a dead rat, in a vase it couldn't climb out of.
Her pastel peach tail is the only color left.
She'd lost herself foraging for crumbs to bring back to her baby.

Momma, you were surviving in the wrong direction,
scavenging for treasure in crumbs left as scraps—
ignoring the burdens that cased you in glass.

## Scene from the Rehab Center

*Dim lights on MOMMA alone at an oval table. She is coloring in a white room, perfectly in line. Her hair swirls into a rhinoceros horn point. In another setting, outside a rehab crisis center, she would look perfectly domestic. The lights brighten the stark basin. There is a box TV playing Emperor's New Groove with a row of fold-out chairs at attention, a phone on a donated side table, and an open wall where nurses check plastic bags for Little Debbie snacks. A few patients are watching the film. One is knitting without technique. One is staring at the DVD player instead of the screen. One laughs at the llama jokes on screen.*

**NURSE**
(entering with POET and AUNTIE) Miss Perkins. You have a visitor.

**MOMMA**
(exploding) HEY, MY BABY! (rushing to hug him).

**POET**
Hey, Momma. How are you?

**MOMMA**
Doing better, doing better—come over here, sit down. Hey, Shawn, good to see you (hugging AUNTIE).

**AUNTIE**
What's up, sis? You're looking good.

**MOMMA**
(still ecstatic, speaking too quickly) Feeling good too. I'm feeling great! How have y'all been?

*All three sit around the stack of coloring books. The POET and his auntie are supportively reserved. They study the room—the smell of Lysol, where the*

> *cardboard walls sag. It is orderly but crowded with fabrications.*

**POET**
Doing well! Ready to graduate soon.

**MOMMA**
(air pumping) Yes! Gra-Du-A-Tion. Super pumped! My baby is graduating.

**POET**
Yes—I'm-

**MOMMA**
When is it, baby? Oh, sorry to cut you off—just so excited!

**POET**
No worries (laughing, but not sure why)—it's May 5th.

**MOMMA**
*May 5th* (she emphasizes it like she's writing it down, but only stares forward with her tightly held cheekbones). I can't believe you're graduating.

> *They all slip into the white noise of the cartoon and air conditioner.*

**AUNTIE**
Thea, you look so much better than you did when we dropped you off, girl. Your hair was sitting straight on top of your head. You looked *a mess*.

**MOMMA**
I was, I was—

**AUNTIE**
I mean you looked (she doesn't finish her sentence but makes a strained hand gesture. It's enough to communicate the point).

**MOMMA**
Mmhhm, I know (nodding emphatically).

**AUNTIE**
Do you remember us bringing you here?

**MOMMA**
Yes! We were lost and I kept asking you not to leave me.

**AUNTIE**
I know—and you kept mumbling to yourself. You just kept saying "Yeah—alright—mhm—yeah" over and over.

**MOMMA**
I was hallucinating! (she says this in the same way you recite a funny story about meeting a celebrity on a plane—she's all smiles).

**POET**
Momma. (his tone kills the fun) We love you. We want you to know how much we love you. We're here for you, we want you to get clean.

**AUNTIE**
Yes, we need you to get clean—get your mind right.

**MOMMA**
(weaponizing her enthusiasm, but behind her silver-lined words there is a howl from a throat walled in scabs, dried blood from meth and enough Patrón to light the Gulf on fire—young too, too young for a mind clotted with brimstone; behind her words, there is a husk from a body made hollow) I got y'all. I'm feeling great! I just needed some time is all.

> *The stage tilts and the performers are momentarily off balance. The play—the masks—have been stilled. Whose line is it? Who's supposed to continue this? The TV is shut off; the nurses and patients start unzipping their costumes.*

```
          I look at Momma and say, We know you can get better.
          I don't want to lie anymore.
```

**MOMMA**
```
That's right—no lies. No lies.
```

No, Momma, I'm serious. We've put this performance up for years. I've known about the drugs since I was 11. I just had no idea it was this bad. Please. I know you can get through this. We love you, and there's no need to pretend anymore.

*Momma's picturesque smile quivers. Within her eyes, a curtain is closing for intermission. She dreams of talking to her mother's tombstone with crickets and dust-rich stones.*

*Grace*, she pleads, *Your Momma needs some extra grace right now.*

**Notes**

The epigraph for the book is from "Creating and Undoing Legacies of Resilience: Black Women as Martyrs in the Black Community Under Oppressive Social Control" by Leah Iman Aniefuna, M. Amari Aniefuna, & Jason M. Williams featured in *Women & Criminal Justice*. Used with permission.

**"Black Mom"** is in the form of a duplex, originated by Jericho Brown.

The quoted names in **"Another Poem About Trayvon Martin"** come from recordings of George Zimmerman's conversations with police.

**"I Miss Your Stories"** is the collection's firstborn. It was the fourth poem I wrote in my life (I was 16).

The poet is not sponsored by or partnered with Twizzlers, Little Debbie snacks, BB Oil Moisturizer, Netflix, or Beyoncé (yet).

The form of **"Howl for Momma Rat"** is a riff on Allen Ginsberg's "Howl," which opens with the lines "I saw the best minds of my generation destroyed by madness, starving / hysterical naked, / dragging themselves through the negro streets at dawn looking for an angry fix."

The handwritten words in **"Church Jewelry and Morning Dead Words"** are from the journal my grandmother wrote in while living with brain cancer. The poem is in the form of a sestina, steadily losing end rhymes.

The left-side content of **"Three Black Sons, Three Black Mothers"** uses articles from *The Greenville News* (1944), *Daily News New York* (Gearty & Gentile, 1986), and *CNN* (Hanna, Lynch, Johnston, Nottingham, & Rose, 2023).

My name is a portmanteau of my family: "Mar-" was my grandmother's childhood nickname; "-Thea-" is my mother's name; "us" represents my aunts and "everyone else." The **"my"** sections were the last written for this book, which is why they are so desperate to escape a last word.

## Gratitude

My warmest appreciation to the editors and curators of the following journals, magazines, and websites where pieces from *The Grace of Black Mothers* previously appeared; best wishes in continuing your work uplifting writers.

*805 Lit + Art*, "Footstool Sister"
*ballast*, "Center, Texas"
*Black Fox Literary Magazine*, "Girl"
*Cathexis Northwest Press*, "An American Dream's Night Stroll"
*Genre: Urban Arts*, "Another Poem About Trayvon Martin"
    & "Southern Hymns"
*HAD*, "Jaden Smith Stole Our Role in *The Karate Kid*"
*Harpy Hybrid Review*, "Optometry with Momma"
    & "Welfare Pirate Queen Code"
*Hoxie Gorge Review*, "Black Mom" & "Sutures in Our Family Photos"
*Longleaf Review*, "Truth is Unpronounceable by Itself"
*Moot Point Magazine*, "Houston, Texas"
*Obsidian: Literature & Arts in the African Diaspora*, "Verdicts"
*On the Run*, "7 Tips for Installing a Cheap Tombstone for Granny
    (Under $639)"
*Sink Hollow Literary Magazine*, "Grace Must Be"
*SoFloPoJo*, "Secret Identity" & "Amazing Grace"
*Spoken Black Girl Magazine*, "The Grace of Black Mothers"
*The Listening Eye*, "Pros and Cons for Keeping the Baby"
*the museum of americana*, "I Miss Your Stories"
*The Progenitor*, "Scholarship Letter"
*The Worcester Review*, "Captions for Pictures We Lost in Storage"
*Voices*, "Family Album," "Swiss Rolls," & "Dominoes"
*Wasteland Review*, "Streaming Dreams Where You Didn't Have the Baby"
    & "Three Black Boys, Three Black Mothers"
*West Trade Review*, "Ode to Toaster Ovens"

Endless hugs to the **Trio House Press** family: Kris for your leadership, Natasha and Ali for your graceful editing, Hadley for being a design magician, Baonhia for the awesome cover design, and the board for your continued support.

B. Broadie bless you for gifting this collection my dream cover art.

To my mentors, Sara Henning, John McDermott, Doug Moore, Peter Streckfus, and Vivek Narayanan,
To my inspirations and North Stars, Sybrina Fulton, Claudia Rankine, Danez Smith, Langston Hughes, Kendrick Lamar, and Nina Simone,
To my newfound readers,
To my first readers and poet sisters, Maya, Taylor, and Katey,
To my ride or dies, Nathan, Kelsey, Ellie, Jason, Syd, Pam, and Eve,
To my aunties, Aunt Na Na, Aunt Jo, Aunt Ena,
and to my mothers, Momma and Ne Ne,
you were behind every word.

**About the Author**

**Martheaus Perkins** was born to a single mother in Center, Texas. After a childhood in and out of homes in Houston, he graduated from Stephen F. Austin State University as a first-generation student. He is the recipient of the Robert Creeley Memorial Award judged by John Keene, the President's Award by *Voices*, the GMU Rinehart Fiction Award, and the Robert Raymond Scholarship. He co-edits *BRAWL Lit* and teaches literature at George Mason University. Currently, he lives in the DMV with fellow writers of the "International House of Poets." The name "Martheaus" is a collection of each woman who helped raise him: "Mar-" for his grandmother's nickname, "-Thea-" for his mother's name, and "-us" for his big aunties.

## About the Artist

Prince George's County, MD Graphic Artist **B. Broadie** fell in love with art when he was a child in elementary school. The moment his teacher gave him a pair of scissors to start cutting shapes, he knew he wanted to create. He still remembers using cotton balls, popsicle sticks, paint, and glitter to create a snowman. He dreamed of having his designs on billboards for people to stop and stare. He was first introduced to digital art in 2005 attending Bowie State University, a Historical Black College (HBCU), majoring in Fine Arts. Through his coursework, Broadie's skills in digital art using photoshop were shaped. While at Bowie State University he took classes in photography, sculpture, and drawing but something about digital art felt natural to him. Broadie shows his love for digital art by blending his skills in graphic design and love of mixed media, bringing about a perfect marriage of his two passions. Broadie's inspiration has been birthed from the richness of Black History, the past, present and possibilities of the future.

In Broadie's own words, "Being a Black Gay male artist from Prince George's County I hope to inspire the future generations of creators by encouraging them to believe in themselves, while going after their dreams. Fully embracing and loving who they are, and to be proud of it. Art has the power to heal, to inspire, and to remind us of the beauty and hope that reside within each of us."

**Artist Statement: About the Cover Art**

Title: Captured Love

Even in bondage, love comforted and gave us HOPE.

During the years of slavery, there was daily buying and selling of children being taken from their enslaved parents. No legal restraints existed on slave owners, who chose to dispose of their "property" however they wanted.

Another time period of state-sanctioned separations was in the 1800s, President Andrew Jackson authorized the Indian Removal Act. Native Americans, mostly youth, were forcibly taken out of their homes and communities and asked to walk for miles to a specially designated "Indian territory." Thousands died on that journey. It has since been named the "Trail of Tears."

The history of separating children from their parents is nothing new in this country.

—B. Broadie

## About the Book

*The Grace of Black Mothers* was designed at Trio House Press through the collaboration of:

Natasha Kane, Primary Editor
Ali Shafer, Supporting Editor
B. Broadie, Cover Art
Baonhia Xiong, Cover Design
Hadley Hendrix, Interior Design

The text is set in Adobe Caslon Pro.

## About the Press

**Trio House Press** is an independent nonprofit press based in Minneapolis, Minnesota. We publish poetry and prose that moves, inspires, and encourages connection, empathy, and understanding, with a special emphasis on underrepresented voices and topics. To find out more about Trio House Press, please visit our website at http://www.triohousepress.org

www.ingramcontent.com/pod-product-compliance
Lightning Source LLC
Chambersburg PA
CBHW060534080526
44586CB00012B/735